Economic Education

THE LIBRARY OF EDUCATION

A Project of The Center for Applied Research in Education, Inc.

G. R. Gottschalk, Director

Categories of Coverage

I	II	III
Curriculum and Teaching	Administration, Organization, and Finance	Psychology for Educators

IV	V	VI
History, Philosophy, and Social Foundations	Professional Skills	Educational Institutions

Economic Education

M. L. FRANKEL

Executive Director
Joint Council on Economic Education

The Center for Applied Research in Education, Inc.
New York

Foreword

Today economic education is a prime concern among thinking people throughout our country. That this is so seems to those who have labored long in the field to be a hope come true. Economic illiteracy has been a continuing concern to educators, business, labor, and agricultural leaders, and government officials for many years. No longer, however, do such leaders have to dissipate their energies in pleading the cause. The "cause" is now every man's "cause." Educators have recognized that progress in our educational system—in fact its very preservation—depends on economic literacy for all citizens. Certainly the leaders of organizations operating in our economy would accept this axiom for their own groups.

A great deal of work has been done in improving economic education in the schools. This book has compiled information that would be helpful to any school system as it considers the steps it wishes to take in developing a program to meet its local needs. For this reason, more than usual emphasis has been given to the "how to do it" aspects of economic education. The problems in developing a school program are detailed and possible solutions to these problems are described. The characteristics of good curriculum development are related to economic education and a bridge is thus established between the content and methods of teaching.

For the guidance of teachers, a breakdown of the grade and subject area placement of economic concepts is given illustrating that economic education can and should be a pervasive theme treated sequentially from Grade 1 through Grade 12.

Also emphasized is the key role which universities and colleges must play in developing the kind of teachers and programs that will lead to an economically literate citizenry. Important suggestions are made on the necessary research and evaluation that must be undertaken for continued success.

v

This book reflects the experiences, the successes, and failures of the Joint Council on Economic Education during the past sixteen years. The author has been actively involved in planning and promoting economic education and brings to the book insights that go far beyond the academic consideration. The philosophy under which the Joint Council operates is clearly delineated, presenting the composite thinking of educational and community leaders who have been actively participating in the program over the years. Their dedication is gratefully acknowledged.

Further, the efforts of the professors of education and economics, deans, school administrators, and teachers whose efforts have provided such a rich store of evidence that economic education can be successfully carried out in the classrooms is deeply appreciated.

MARTIN ESSEX
Superintendent of Schools
Akron, Ohio

Economic Education

M. L. Frankel

This volume on economic education outlines a new development in American education which began with the establishment of the Joint Council on Economic Education in 1948. It is a complementary volume to others in the Library of Education such as *The Social Studies, Trends and Issues in Secondary Education,* and *Elementary School Teaching Practices.* Economic education is an important and growing area in the education of children, youth, and adults.

The book emphasizes practices in economic education today, the need for economic understanding, and the development of school programs at all school levels. It gives specific help on curriculum development to the busy teacher and school administrator. The role of economics as a discipline is discussed. The responsibilities of colleges and universities for the education of teachers in economic education are clearly stated. The book is concluded with a chapter on the need for further research and evaluation.

The author is well qualified to write in the field of economic education. His vocation is economic education as executive director of the agency which is doing so much in curriculum development and in-service education of teachers. He has made this book significant by stating the principles of economic education, describing on-going programs, and pointing to needed improvements in the future.

WALTER A. ANDERSON
Content Editor

Contents

CHAPTER I

Economic Education Today

Kalamazoo, Michigan

"What is that big machine doing in the schoolyard?" This question provided an occasion for a group of second-grade children to cluster about the window in the classroom and satisfy an immediate curiosity. But it also was the occasion for a gifted teacher in the Kalamazoo, Michigan, schools to sense quickly the possibilities of capitalizing on the interest of these children. As in many schools across the nation, second-grade work in the social studies centers around the community. There was a relationship between the machine in the schoolyard, and especially the operating engineer, and the understanding of the community through its helpers. *Men and Machines Work Together* was the resulting study.[1]

The machine, a ditch digger, began its work. Repairs had to be made in the wall of the school gymnasium, and children at this age are probably the most avid sidewalk superintendents that can be found. Numerous questions were raised. "How does it work?" "Who owns it?" "Why don't men dig the hole?" "Who is the man in the machine?" "Where did he get it?" are but samples.

Classroom discussion led to a visit by the class to the schoolyard and a conversation with the operator. The efficiency of the machine and its relation to the cost of the job were brought out. The cost of the machine underlined the investment of the owner-operator based on savings, and the services of the bank as the remaining source of capital were examined. The bank thus became the second community resource for the study. The purpose of the visit to the bank was to gain an understanding of the bank and the relation of a loan to the money deposited by the children and other citizens of the community. In this way, the bank was identified as a source of capital investment for many projects in the city. The concept of interest as a return on investment of capital was established.

---

[1] Mildred Borton, *Men and Machines Work Together* (Minneapolis: Curriculum Resources, Inc., 1961).

1

Pursuing the importance of the machine and the contributions of technological advances to the well-being of the community resulted in studying the uses of tools in the home. The use of the needle, screwdriver, hammer, telephone, and light bulbs were demonstrated. Improvement in productivity resulting from the use of such tools was discussed, and the contribution of the individual using the tool to its efficiency was not overlooked.

Gradually, the discussion led to a consideration of the work done by parents. Many occupations were listed, and the class decided to investigate these occupations to find out just what their parents did. Visits, on an individual student basis, were made to many businesses and industries in town. Several of the parents came to class to explain what they did to earn a living. The individual operator-owner concept was projected to the highly specialized manufacturing plant. The contributions of each gainfully employed person were assessed in terms of his contribution to the community. Production of goods and services, earnings, machines in the production process, productivity, technological innovation and the factors bringing about greater innovation, distribution of benefits of increased productivity, and the handicaps caused by lack of machinery in many countries were among the topics studied.

West Hartford, Connecticut

In West Hartford, Connecticut, a study by a sixth-grade class[2] indicated the necessity for economic growth in their geographical area. For example, the growth of population in the community and all of the problems the community faced in providing additional and adequate educational facilities were examined, such as split sessions, temporary quarters, and other stopgap measures. The grumblings and complaints called for an answer. This was a personal dislocation, and the students were entitled to an explanation. Again, we see the motivation for a meaningful investigation in the area of economics. The study revealed that growth in the community is affected by individual action and that the individual is affected by growth. Natural and human resources played a major role. Sources of capital

---

[2] Miriam E. Silcox, "Economic Life of Hartford," *Economic Education Experiences of Enterprising Teachers* (New York: Joint Council on Economic Education, 1963), p. 45.

investment were needed. Individual enterprise was a key to the development. Growth in West Hartford had to be associated with growth in the entire Hartford area, in Connecticut itself, in New England, and the nation. The factors of economic growth are the same in each of the geographical areas. The study also showed the interdependence of people in the community, the state, and the nation.

Interviews of town officials were conducted concerning the actions that were being taken to meet the challenge of growth and why it was impossible to institute certain remedies. Planning specialists came to the class along with local tax officials to explain their projections. The Chamber of Commerce officers were questioned on steps which they were taking to meet the challenge. Officials of manufacturing establishments and other businesses contributed insights into possible expansion plans.

The resources, after they were all investigated, the organizational patterns, and the effectiveness of West Hartford in meeting the growth were compared to problems which other communities were facing. The study was taken beyond national boundaries, and comparisons were made with areas in Latin America. Using the factors involved in the analysis of growth, the students were able to reach conclusions on the reasons and opportunities either for or against growth in other areas. The question of why better use was not made of the available resources was raised, especially in regard to the Latin American countries. The students had come a long way from a concern with personal dislocation to an investigation of community and area development in their own as well as in other nations.

Paterson, New Jersey

What does a teacher tell a thirteen-year old boy when he asks, "Why did my father have to get a new job?" Terry Anderson, in the eighth grade of the Woodrow Wilson Junior High School in Paterson, New Jersey, wanted to know, "Why have so many textile mills in the Passaic Valley closed?" His father had been employed in one of those mills as a skilled machinist and was having a difficult time adjusting to his new job in another factory located some distance from home. Terry had a right to know *how* to find the answer and to understand *why* such displacements occurred.

Lucky Terry, his teacher was willing to help. There was a time when Terry's teacher would have had either to ignore his question, offer a superficial explanation, or, most disastrous of all, given him an incorrect, emotional, biased response.

But now it was different. Terry's teacher discussed with the class the seriousness of the problem in the Passaic Valley and asked if they would like to look into the problem further. When they voted yes, the class organized itself into committees. The problem had to be defined clearly. Its relationship to the big problem of economic growth and security had to be understood.

The class went to work. The youngsters visited executives of several textile mills. They called on labor officials and the Chamber of Commerce. They studied new industries in the area, and learned why these industries had been attracted to the Passaic Valley. The class sought, too, to determine the importance of international trade to the area. Soon they were probing into the problems facing the United States in relation to the European Common Market.

And the young investigators got help from the whole community. Materials from a variety of organizations and other sources were made available. The teacher showed films and filmstrips dealing with the major problems of industrial obsolescence, international trade, and conditions favorable to economic growth.

The youngsters began to ask questions. What alternative courses of economic action could be taken in the Passaic Valley area? What would be the consequence of these alternatives? They examined. They discussed. Economic education was a reality at the Woodrow Wilson Junior High School.

Minneapolis, Minnesota

"Have you been watching and listening for 'Economics In The News'?"[3] This is how a teacher greeted the fifth- and sixth-graders in a Minneapolis School in March, 1963. The radio program started with an examination of the headlines dealing with economics and a simple quiz. The radio commentator then reviewed the meaning of economics. Economics as "choice-making" was related to problems of youngsters in the fifth and sixth grade. The alternatives of

[3] One of a series of broadcasts prepared by the Minneapolis Economic Education Committee for local educational radio programs.

spending or saving with available resources were highlighted. Scarcity of resources in relation to our wants and the relationship of interdependence and specialization to the scarcity factor were illustrated.

The need for goods and services paved the way for the radio commentator to explain the market system with money as a medium of exchange.

Continuing into a study of geography based on news items, attention was focused on President Kennedy's trip in December, 1961 to Latin America. The "Alliance for Progress" was explained and its economic underpinnings analyzed.

Using headlines as a basis, the commentator discussed the displacement of workers in Australia, an atomic energy-producing plant in Minnesota, a story about color Polaroid, and finally the invention of "protein powder" in England. The students were constantly confronted with the commentator's question "What economic facts are involved in these news items?"

A Ninth-Grade Class

A ninth-grade class in civics, studying the political organization and problems of their own community and area, realized quickly that a political study of the community was incomplete without an economic study. A question had been raised which was sobering to the entire class, "Why was employment high in our area compared to the employment in the distressed areas as reported periodically by the Area Redevelopment Administration?"

The teacher recognized that the community's economic life was but a microcosm of the total American economy. The community provides the same topics for investigation; its institutions and activities are similar to those on the national scene.

Basic to the study was a recognition by the student that full and improved production is necessary to maintain an increasing standard of living. This in turn guarantees a supply and variety of products enabling the individual to exercise his freedom of choice as a consumer.

The students studied economic operations that were basic. The community study provided the opportunity for active inquiry. The study proceeded into how the economy of the area functioned to meet the needs of the people. The class then examined the resources and technical development of the area in relation to their influence on the economy. The ideas behind economic activity were explored as were the institutions for economic activity as a means of activating the ideas and not as ends in themselves. Using the local situation as a base, the factors of productivity, distribution, business organization, individual competence, purchasing power, capital formation, and government policing were examined in detail.

The investigation then considered the relation of the economy with the ideals and standards of values of the community. Goals were determined from a survey of adults in the community as well as from class members. Much stress was laid on the importance of considering all the alternative courses of action possible and the effect of each on the goals sought. And finally, the students were brought face to face with the individual's role, by his action and thought, in improving the economy.

A semester's study enabled the students to clearly see themselves as a responsible part of the continuing health of the economy of their community. They had the opportunity to see the economy operate at first hand and to learn of the motivation required to continue its well-being. They were "observing," using the community as a laboratory, the day-to-day activities of the economy and what made it "tick."

A Vermont High School

"As a teacher of typing, shorthand, and transcription in a small rural school (Vermont)[4] where an economics course is not taught, I propose to use a series of letters, each one a reply to some hypothetical question relating to some problem of economic understanding." Thus, a business education teacher's purpose was clearly stated. Stenography classes were to be used for developing vocabulary and discussing subject matter. The transcription letters would enable the typists to think rather than to just copy. Reading assignments gave direction to the work going on in the classroom.

Through the medium of dictation and transcription, money and its role in the economy could be discussed, and the deposit and crea-

---

[4] Phyllis Farrow, *Creating An Awareness of Economic Principles Through A Series of Transcription Letters* (New York: Joint Council on Economic Education, 1961).

tion of credit functions of banking were explained. The function of the Federal Reserve System in controlling credit through its reserve requirement powers was among other understandings developed through what was heretofore only a "skill" subject.

Indianola, Iowa

At Indianola, Iowa, a teacher of American History, reviewing his work for the year, was intrigued by a student's question about the period from the Civil War to 1900. "What influenced businessmen to make the decisions they made during that period?" The teacher was struck by the importance of the question and in the next school year introduced a unit on the role of business in the life of America. The study led to new subject areas, and relationships were found with the changing family structure, urbanization, increasing government involvement in the economy, the development of labor unions, and the determination of political platforms.

A new respect for the private enterprise system was developed, and students saw the importance of the profit motive in improving the standard of living of the people. Historically, the students saw the changes in business structure—the dominance of the corporation, the change in size as it related to the change in size of the nation, and the development of a managerial class. Through the studies that have been made of businesses, small numbers of companies were seen as pace setters, increasing in size and influence. Mass production was recognized as part of the production and technological revolution and that mass production in turn fostered mass distribution. Such changes necessitated the growth of big business. Diversification could be recognized even during the late 1800's and the reasons for it were checked with national producers in Iowa. The problem of elimination of competition was also investigated, but in its proper historical context.

The "captains of industry" became a focus of study, and the newly developed research materials by historians and social scientists were brought into the classroom. The comparison of the research of people like the noted political historian Allan Nevins to the accounts in the textbooks proved to be explosive. The concept of ownership was also pursued to modern times where today 2,000,000 shareholders in one company are now a reality. Financial institutions, mutual funds, and pension funds were seen as sources of capital investment.

New concepts resulted from the investigations of the class. These concepts concerned productivity and production, the centering of economic power in few hands, the development of a new type of competition, and the increased attention to prohibiting and regulating monopolies. The distribution of income as an historical development was plotted as supporting evidence in reassessing the role of business.

The students had learned their history, but it now was alive. They had learned what had made the history. They looked at the decisions made as turning points in American life. What at one time seemed correct values attached to studies like *The Muckrakers* were reconsidered in light of the goals of growth, stability, security, freedom and justice. As one student put it, "What seemed to be simple yes or no answers turned out to be complex ones. We had to stop, think again, and develop new answers."

Urbana, Illinois

In an economics course at University High School in Urbana, Illinois, the class became concerned with the problem of economic growth. They recognized its importance as something that could not be taken for granted. In the course of their study they decided that as a class they should develop their own *Policy Statement on Economic Growth.*[5] Pupil-teacher planning led the class to certain procedures. A classroom library of as many materials as possible had to be developed. The librarian, the University Department of Economics, national organizations, and publishers provided the source for multiple types of materials. Visual presentations—films, flannel boards, charts and graphs—were developed and consultants were brought in frequently. Since Chicago was a center for committee activities in working with community resources, the Federal Reserve Bank, major industrial plants, labor headquarters, and the offices of the farm organizations supplemented the resources of the University. Role-playing was introduced. Evaluation was a continuing part of the study.

---

[5] *Policy Statement on Economic Growth* (Urbana, Illinois: University High School, December 17, 1962).

The students' report concerned itself with the importance of growth to the American and international economies. The record of growth was plotted and illustrated. The factors which determined the rate of growth were fully investigated, including the natural, human and man-made resources, investment, demand, and the social and political environment. The goals of the economy were studied and analyzed in connection with the growth rate, and the inevitable conflicts between them were recognized as part of the political decision-making.

As a final step, the class presented its "policy recommendations" on natural resources, unemployment, research, education, development and mobility of resources, investment, demand, and the political and social environment. They concluded that more capital investment was needed in areas other than consumption and leisure. Education, research, and development, they felt, should receive a much greater proportion of the Gross National Product.

But the policy statement was not unanimous. Dissents were presented on the section dealing with demand and on the section dealing with the removal of government subsidies to agriculture. The students wrote their own texts in a style that exhibited the best of classroom methods and a grasp of knowledge far beyond that possessed by most adults. The enthusiasm of the students and the parents was due to the realization that they were engaged in something vital. They were in a position to evaluate decisions being made at all levels of government and by private sources as well.

How were these teachers able to handle the questions which had been raised by their students? How were they able to take the routine classes and courses which they were teaching and breathe new life into them? The answer is that they had received a special kind of supplementary education in economics designed just for teachers. They received this in carefully planned workshops, seminars, discussion-lecture series, and a variety of other in-service programs conducted under the auspices of a Council on Economic Education in their area. There, the teachers attended sessions dealing with economic problems and their application to their classrooms. Professors of economics, education, and geography were brought in to discuss the various factors which influenced the problems in economics that were part of their regular classroom work. Experts on economic growth, international trade, business development, economic history, resource use, and labor, among others, were present at various times to contribute to this background. Representatives from business, industry, labor and government supplemented the remarks of the academic experts. What seemed to be national and international concerns up to that time were related to the area and the local scene.

In all, the educational experiences had provided teachers with confidence in their ability to teach economics, because they had learned the subject matter of economics along with successful ways of teaching it.

The economic education programs for these teachers, and ultimately their students, were no accident. The Councils on Economic Education in these respective areas had organized these programs for teachers to meet the requests which had come from schools and teachers. The State Council helped to develop the programs with their cooperating universities and colleges. Their field directors visited the schools and worked with the teachers. The Councils identified the university professors who would participate effectively and set up the panels of businessmen, labor leaders and civic officials. A solid base of acceptance had been, and continues to be, developed as a result of the many programs that Councils conduct for educators. Economists, curriculum specialists, and teachers have had experiences that have stimulated continued school program improvement and brought about the demands for economic education that now exist.

Councils on Economic Education

State Councils, like those which made possible the classroom projects described above, have been established throughout the country. The community leaders that constitute those councils, along with the educators, have put their faith in economic education rather than economic advocacy. These independent, self-financed state, regional, and community councils are affiliates of the Joint Council on Economic Education. The Joint Council is the national headquarters and clearinghouse for an all out attack on the problem of economic illiteracy. It is this organization, and only this one, that has the close affiliation and cooperation of the American Economic Association, the regional Economic Associations, and the major professional groups of the National Education Association in carrying out its program. It is the only organization in the field that is supported and assisted by national business, labor, agricultural, research, and government organizations.

The program which the Joint Council on Economic Education has developed in support of the American economy is characterized by the following principles subscribed to by educators.[6]

A. The viewpoints of all the major sectors of the economy—agriculture, government, business, labor, the consumer—must receive full consideration in the formulation of programs and in the development of materials.

B. When advisory committees or councils are used, such groups should include representatives from agriculture, business, government, and labor, as well as from education.

C. Leadership in the field of economic education, as in all areas of education, should be in the hands of the educators.

D. Economic education should encourage study of:
1. The concepts and principles of economics
2. Economic institutions
3. Economic activities
4. Economic problems

E. The study of economic problems should be conducted within the framework of:
1. Maximum objectivity
2. Complete freedom of inquiry and discussion

F. The school in its instructional program in economics should take no political position nor support any special point of view.

G. The preparation and selection of classroom and home study materials should be based on criteria that conform to the principles listed above.

H. Educators should hold to the view that no one textbook infallibly prescribes all the right answers to economic problems. This means that no one textbook should be regarded as so "all right" that no other textbook would be acceptable. Information for class use should be obtained from a variety of sources representing a variety of viewpoints.

I. The continuous growth and development of economic education must rest upon a plan for regular reexamination and revision of programs for the preparation of teachers and for continuously providing in-service programs for teachers.

---

[6] Joint Council on Economic Education, *Report of the Economic Education Committee of the Southern States Work Conference* (New York: Joint Council on Economic Education, 1961).

The fact that the youth in many areas of America today are receiving improved economic education stems from the unique Joint Council program that has been in operation since 1948. This planned program has resulted in a new dimension being added to class studies throughout the school sequence from the kindergarten to the twelfth grade and serves as a basis for this publication.

CHAPTER II

Need for Economic Understanding

Rationale for Economic Understanding

Today men know that economic institutions are not divinely ordained or inspired. They know that the degree of freedom that exists and the economic security that each possesses is the result of deliberate creative effort. The realization that man, in large part, controls his own economic destiny had led to social revolutions and rapid evolutions. Man has developed several systems of social organization and their differences, in the main, can be found in the economic foundations of each.

The essential distinction between the economy of the United States and the major competing systems is that, in the United States, the ultimate responsibility for policy decisions, including economic policy, rests with the citizens. This is not an empty shibboleth. This is a fact.

A brief examination of some of our nation's economic gains over the last fifty years is in order:

1. The output per worker has grown rapidly. Total production has more than tripled in the last four decades and there is every indication that it will continue to increase strongly.
2. The goods produced are distributed much more widely than ever before.
3. The economy has operated to develop a large middle class and public policies have been adopted which tend to make for a more equitable distribution of wealth.
4. The economies of the nations of the world have reached a point where any action in one nation sets off a chain reaction in the economy of the United States, demonstrating the extent of international interdependence today.

Economists point out that in achieving these advances the American people developed many new products and created investment opportunities for all. The economy of abundance has brought sharp reflection on the desirability of the present allocation of the resources of the country. Machinery has been created to control the volume of expenditures, but concern is being exhibited in determining expenditures for what purpose. The economy has brought about greater concentration of economic units, but the economy has also grown more competitive, asserting itself not only in price but also in design, production, and service.

As a people our citizens have legislated "built-in stabilizers" which make our economy less susceptible to the severe ups and downs so characteristic of other eras. But the correcting of some of the shortcomings has simply given rise to new problems in an ever developing cycle of what may be termed the heart of economics, a constant resolving of the dilemma of unlimited wants and limited resources. The history of the development of our economy is studded with gains, but these did not occur through chance. They are the composite result of individual, group, and governmental decisions. And the future quality of such decisions will determine whether this nation and the world will progress, stagnate, or retrogress economically. The future is controlled by the economic decisions of our citizens. Economic education, which makes possible increasingly wise citizen decisions, therefore, is essential to the survival of our free society.

Economics provides the substance which is at the heart of most political questions that require decisions by citizens, and a bit of reflection or examination will indicate that economics is a behavioral science created by man and controlled by man. For these reasons, it becomes a necessity and an obligation for citizens to gain a basic understanding of the operation of the American economy in order to be better equipped to play a positive role in the formulation of vital decisions of the body politic.

Individual citizens determine national policies by what they do or do not do. Collectively, they determine the decisions made in the area of economic policy. But intelligent decisions can be made only when people understand economic considerations and weigh the consequences and implications of alternative courses of action.

Not every citizen is required to be an economist with the full learning of the profession, but American society will prosper in the world today in direct proportion to the economic understanding of the members of that society.

Essentially, what is being discussed here is the importance of citizens facing the significant issues which confront the society in which they live, and, at the same time, developing techniques for attacking and resolving them. Economic education offers the perfect medium to help accomplish this goal.

To summarize: In the free society and economic system of this nation the decisions of individual citizens, acting independently and collectively, determine the direction of the economy. If those decisions are informed and wise, the nation will prosper. If they are based on emotion, prejudice, and ignorance, the nation will stagnate and collapse. The function of economic education is to assist our citizens to make those economic decisions that foster best the attainment of the American goals of economic growth, stability, security, freedom, and justice.

It is precisely because of the rationale above that the schools have a key role to play. Entrusted with the responsibility of preparing students to enter the adult world of citizenship and the world of work, programs must be devised which reflect a sustained and continuous effort to assist the student to develop a basic understanding of economics. As an area of study, economic education lends itself admirably to the educational program. The development of economic literacy should start at an early age in a child's career. Concepts which illustrate the introduction of basic essentials of the American economy, such as specialization, division of labor, interdependence, production and consumption activities of people, freedom of job selection, job security, capital formation and expenditures, taxes, and the importance of human and natural resources, provide the basis for a child's economic model easily introduced from the first grade, as illustrated by the classroom descriptions in Chapter I. This is not specialized education but general in nature, introduced into the already existing units of teaching. By successive experiences at each grade level there will come a time, compatible with the child's maturity, when a degree of specialization will be necessary. But this illustrates the flexibility of economic education and the ease with which it may be integrated into many units and subjects.

No discipline in the school curriculum lends itself to a greater variety of teaching methods than does economics. "Problem solving" is inherent in the very nature of the subject. This encourages critical and creative thinking. Every day experiences of the student provide the starting point for economic education. There is less sheer "knowing" than "knowing about," because economics involves all the media of communication in its study. In addition the community provides the laboratory for investigation and research. Such activity can only serve to bring the school and community closer together.

Of major concern are the present and future needs of the learner. Past experiences are not worth much unless they are used as a base for a thorough analysis of today's problems. These problems are different from those of the past, but the analytical process used is the same. Economic education, therefore, by its very dynamic quality, forces both teacher and learner into the realities of today's society.

And finally, economics is of immediate importance because teachers who are now dealing with youth face a whole new set of individual differences in terms of their economic backgrounds. There are some in whose families there may be an affiliation with a union, an executive group, a farm, or a government agency. Families as consuming units influence the economic indicators. Some students may be in school because the social security program makes it possible. Others may be present because the job market dictates that they remain in school in order to acquire the additional preparation now being demanded as part of the electronic and energy revolution. Whatever the causes may be, the effect is directly related to economic conditions and demands.

Schools are recognizing that they do have a responsibility to equip the students with the necessary learning to successfully be creative on the one hand and adaptable on the other to a society that is motivated to a large extent by economic demands. Economic analysis will not solve, in isolation, the problems which the nation and the world face. This only serves, however, to emphasize that studied alone, economics will not make the contribution that it must make to more intelligent thinking.

Above all, the schools must accept the challenge of restoring responsibility to the decision-making process. Responsibility and objectivity are synonymous, one operating in the political, economic, and social arena of direct action, and the other in reflective thinking in intellectual affairs. Both are brought about by definite social arrangements. Those who make decisions must answer for them to those who are affected by the decisions. Those affected by social decisions have to possess the ability to ask relevant questions, know whom to ask, exercise enough power for their questions to be taken seriously, and have some measure of free choice.

Closely linked to the responsibility of the individual is the desire on the part of all in a society for freedom, the opposite side of the coin. People possess freedom to the extent that they are in a position to make an effective choice from a number of alternatives. This is not simple for the words "effective" and "alternatives" require a degree of sophistication in an individual if free choice is to prevail. Freedom is paradoxical, since today it is expanded by the very fact of society's dictum to curtail it. But freedom makes no concession to any deviation from freedom to seek the truth.

Responsibility and freedom cannot be separated from economic understanding. The classroom illustrations in Chapter I and those referred to in other chapters were developed with these ends in mind. Similarly, they were concerned with problems that are of a persistent nature in economic life. A look at these would throw light on the characteristics of a good school program as well.

Problems of a Persistent Nature in our Economic Life

Edwin G. Nourse's article, "The Persistent Problems of the American Economy" has given educators a useful guide.[1] In it, the problems have been classified under the headings of natural resources, the labor force, the need for capital, forms of business organization and management, and government and economic life.

In each of the categories there is an historical context within which the problem must be viewed. From such a vantage point, one begins to see not only the persistent nature of the problems, but also the fact that the problems have not been solved. Evident from the brief analysis of each problem presented is a continuous process of social change which, in turn, reflects itself in a change of personalities within the society. Hagen develops this relationship and concludes that problem-solving is the mechanism which produces the creative individual who constantly directs his energies to attacking the

---

[1] Edwin G. Nourse, "The Persistent Problems of the American Economy," *Social Education*, Vol. 17 (November 1953), 297–311. Reprinted by the Joint Council on Economic Education.

problem.[2] In his book, the creative person is defined as one who:

1. Is unconsciously alert to the new aspects of the phenomena
2. Sees the phenomena as forming an understandable and manageable system
3. Encounters new aspects of the problem which leads to new understanding, not frustration
4. Responds imaginatively to new stimuli that the new observations provide
5. Mentally deals with the substance of the problem rather than the frustrating reactions
6. Reflects in the conscious process the results of the unconscious thinking process
7. Is attracted by problem-solving and is constantly trying to accomplish more
8. Escapes from his anxiety by his creative effort motivated by a duty to achieve

The persistent problems, therefore, provide the case studies not from a detached vantage point but from a point of recognition of the problem and the efforts made to solve it, the recognition of a temporary solution creating additional phenomena and the process of tackling these at the present moment through an action program. To illustrate, Nourse sets forth as a basic problem in the natural resource area the question of property rights in relation to conserving and developing these resources. The degree of private ownership running through the spectrum to government ownership provides the alternative solutions. As a case in point the following illustration is pertinent.

> Grazing Resources. The problem of conserving and administrating grazing lands runs far back in our history and is interrelated with the adjacent problem of agriculture on one side and forestry on the other. Private livestock interests, in the absence of regulation, greatly impaired this resource through overgrazing and no reseeding. The Taylor Grazing Act of 1934 undertook to organize a long-run conservation and redevelopment program, with practices largely defined and self-administered by existing livestock organizations, merely coordinated by Federal and state grazing officials. The present policy appears to be that of keeping submarginal agricultural lands available for grazing on reasonable terms of ownership or lease, of making effective use of the grazing potentialities of timber reservations as justified by prevailing cost and price relationships.

---

[2] Everett E. Hagen, *On The Theory of Social Change* (Homewood, Ill.: Dorsey Press, Inc., 1963), pp. 87–96.

Controversy develops as to what is technically possible or economically feasible and how the cost and benefits shall be divided between private and public agencies and among livestock interests.[3]

Or, in another area, namely the "Need for Capital," the problem of "Private Capitalism vs. Government Capitalism" is brought into focus.

> Actual experience under free government has taught us that a good practical answer to the problem of capital formation is found by having part of our capital needs furnished through the public treasury—Federal, state, and local. Some people have come to think that the whole problem would be handled better if practically all of this function were turned over to the state, if we nationalized our basic industries and had a system of state socialism or even communism. Clearly this would change the form of our business institutions and practices, but the basic problem of getting just the right amount of capital at the right times and places would still persist. Likewise, the problem of deciding how to divide the total product so as to satisfy consumers, workers, and capital suppliers would be just as real and possibly more difficult of workable settlement. There is wisdom in a multitude of bargainers, whereas centralized control carries the possibility of monumental mistakes.[4]

A clear distinction is made in selecting these major problem areas between what are the basic problems and the customary problems dealt with in the school. Inflation, labor-management relations, farm income, consumer choice, urban redevelopment can rightly be termed *clusters of problems,* as similarly, housing, medicare, gold flow, highways, and railroads may be termed *symptoms of problem areas. Where* the start is made by the teacher and the school is of no great material difference. What is of great importance is that the student is led from the starting point. To recognize that an analytical economic problem, as organized in Nourse's framework, is very different from a socioeconomic problem involving political, sociological, and psychological implications, is a task to be accomplished in the learning process. Relationships must be clearly shown functionally and as magnitudes of one area associated with alternative magnitudes of the political, social, and psychological areas.

---

[3] Nourse, *op. cit.,* p. 301.
[4] *Ibid.,* p. 307.

Concepts Involved

Out of an understanding of the persistent problems, and implicit in the understanding of each, are some overriding concepts which may be termed *goals* or *aims*. One could easily list them as attitudes to be developed in the classroom as well, for they constitute a framework within which all citizens operate in this society, and, therefore, are of great relevance to the school curriculum. Initially, there is a recognition that, basically, man's wants are relatively simple. They may be summed up as a desire for the esteem of one's fellow, a reasonable amount of security for one's self and family, freedom to develop culturally and express one's self spiritually, the opportunity to improve by one's own efforts, and a feeling of belonging, of working cooperatively to build a better life. These desires have been with the American citizen from the very beginning. The complexity of contemporary life, however, has amplified these basic wants and changed the form of expression of desires for such things as security, educational opportunity, and stability of employment. The politico-economic problems of the day are those that deal with these very factors. In a larger sense, an effort is being made to achieve a greater equality within society without destroying democratic values, to improve the urge for creative work, create an environment for change, and for making a greater provision for a fair competitive spirit.

The citizen today must meet certain challenges to fulfill the desires mentioned above. These challenges may be described as participation in the formulation of policy, knowledge sufficient to allow for an intelligent approach to policy formulation, a constant upgrading of abilities, a recognition that life today requires the citizen to assume multiple roles in his activities, and an ability to adjust to a life that requires a high degree of mobility, flexibility, fluidity, and adaptability.

All of these can be achieved through a study of economics in the schools. Specifically the goals of economic study are:

1. *A recognition that a decision in any sector of the economy affects the whole economy.* Policy is formulated at this level. The individual is forced to recognize that he is an integral part of the system, and in seeking his own improvement contributes to the improvement of all of society. Individual decision-making, however,

must always proceed on the basis that the consequences of such decisions must be considered in light of their effects on society.

> At Vincennes, Indiana, a study of National Income Accounting at the tenth-grade level, introduced the idea of the interrelatedness of all economic activities by utilizing the familiar circular-flow charts, with money payments (which become money income, which become money payments, etc.) going around in one direction and the goods and services (which become producer goods, which become consumer goods, etc.) going around in the opposite direction. The student can easily see how his individual decisions affect the dollar flow when the aggregate decisions of people are consolidated.[5]

2. *The facing of alternatives with sophistication derived from an adequate background of knowledge.* This presupposes that each person will discipline himself to an analytical process of reasoning (this will be described fully in Chapter V). A free economy does not involve a dogmatic approach but, in reality, one of trial and error where each new situation must be faced in the light of the relevant facts and the changing alternatives. The entire concept of individual and governmental action for the general welfare, the degree of participation of each, is important here and is described in the illustration "Grazing Resources."

> At the level of the individual at a grade school in New Haven, the teacher of the second grade recognizing the need to introduce economic understanding to youngsters who came from low-income families, introduced a unit on money. This was related to the needs of the family and then to the concept of money as a scarce resource. The exercise entitled "If I Had a Dollar" led to a simple understanding of the law of opportunity cost and the law of diminishing returns. Such questions by the teacher as, "What would happen if more and more of the dimes you have were used to buy any one product such as candy, toys or clothes?" begins the early process of analytical thinking. The experiences in the classroom provided the trial and error and here the beginnings of the market as an allocator of resources is exploited. For higher grade levels the sum of money could be increased in the exercises used. The same concepts are developed, however.[6]

3. *The realization that increased production is the key to more*

---

[5] Sister Mary Joanita, "National Income Accounting," *Economic Education Experiences of Enterprising Teachers* (New York: Joint Council on Economic Education, 1963), pp. 26–27.

[6] Florence Leventhal, "Exercises on Handling Scarce Resources," *Economic Education Experiences of Enterprising Teachers, op. cit.,* pp. 81–84.

*products and that satisfying the desire for one product may negate
achieving another desire.* Resources used for one product cannot be
used for another in most instances. A sense of relationships is established here and an understanding of the unity of the economy is
developed. Every economic problem is related to the conflict between unlimited wants and limited resources; and economic issues
often arise even when the phenomena dealt with appear to be noneconomic in character. The citizen "will face such choices as those
between alternative satisfactions, between present and future goods,
between alternative methods of production, between production and
leisure, between stability and security and innovation and progress,
and between the market and group action, under whatever conditions and guides these choices may appear, with some slight degree
of sophistication—with a sense of confident awareness. He will have
perspective. . . ."[7]

In Winnetka, Illinois, an eleventh-grade teacher and his class
demonstrated to the Mid-West Economics Association the function-
ing of the American economy, present trends influencing growth
and stability, and how private and public policies contribute to a
growing and stable economy. The teacher used the students' concern
about the problem of finding jobs and their desire for an increasing
standard of living to lead into the problem of how to maintain a
growing and stable economy in the United States. The class first
studied the problem of economic growth. Two committees investigated the historical and economic forces contributing to economic
growth. The "historical" committee listed one by one such positive
forces as: the lack of aristocratic tradition; the mobility of social
classes; the immigrants' philosophy of getting ahead; the decentral-
ization of initiative; free public education; and the desire for economic advancement. The "economic" committee looked into the
factors contributing to economic growth: the availability of resources; the size, skill, and mobility of the labor force; the sources
and availability of capital for new plant and equipment, and the
attitude of American business which accepts new ideas and is ready
to reorganize existing resources to achieve increasing efficiency.
The class then examined the historical development of economic
growth through the study of the Gross National Product and the
National Income. They recognized that although this growth has
sustained an upward trend, it has been interrupted by inflations and
deflations. These ups and downs, they discovered, have been caused

---

[7] Ben Lewis, "On Economic Understanding," *Economics in General Education*
(New York: Joint Council on Economic Education, 1954), p. 27.

largely by disturbances in the relationship between income flow and flow of goods and services.

The class then reorganized itself to represent the various segments of the American economy—consumers, business, government, financial institutions, and the Federal Reserve System. Each reported on the future intentions of the segment it represented. "Consumers" reported whether they will increase or decrease government expenditures and whether it will balance the budget or aim toward a surplus or a deficit; and "financial institutions" on the credit policy they plan to pursue. Following these reports the committee representing the Federal Reserve System discussed the financial measures they could introduce to assure stability, and the "government" committee presented a program to support the Federal Reserve System in this effort. Certainly the students were left with a sense of perspective. Choice making by a variety of interests were studied and the process examined.

4. *An appreciation of the contributions made by diverse groups to the totality of production and a recognition that productive effort requires a continual upgrading of the labor force.* Education is looked upon as a continuous process. The complex, dynamic character of the economy needs to be understood. The search for talent is a critical one in an industrialized society. The dependence on research and technology for a thriving economy must be realized. The shift from production of goods to service occupations as the major source of employment opportunities has deep implications for society and for education in particular. Manpower usage spills over into what may, on the surface, seem to be political or social problems.

At Temple City, California, a program has been established which builds upon actual work experience and the economic realities which underlie those experiences. In the ninth grade, study concentrates on the work opportunities, job requirements, vocational and educational goals, and individual counseling on student programs leading to occupational activities. Field studies are conducted for orientation purposes.

In the last three years work experience for compensation is provided and focuses "on the education of each youth in understanding himself and his abilities, the world of work and the free enterprise system."[8] Classroom study concentrates on business in the Los Angeles area at the tenth grade, state and national economics and

---

[8] *Preliminary Guide* (Temple City, Calif.: Temple City Unified School District, 1963), p. 2.

its influence on the local scene in the eleventh grade, and international economics and world affairs in the twelfth grade.

The study leads from the personal objectives of the student to a consideration of the characteristics necessary for success and the requirements for employment in today's world of work. Future projections of job opportunities are analyzed. The role of the consumer is analyzed following this introductory study, and this serves as a lead into the nature of economic problems which follow the pattern set by the Iowa Primer series.[9] Eventually this leads back to developing a knowledge of the factors that tend to govern employment, characteristics of employment, economic factors of the job, and the dignity of labor. Each succeeding year builds on the base described above. This is one school's answer to achieving the fourth goal above.[10]

5. *The acceptance of the fact that economic life involves a rational living together as humans; that people adjust to changing roles as they live as citizens and as members of different groups.* In a single day, a person may be a consumer, producer, and distributor. He may be an employee or employer operating in the private or public sector. He is thus forced to consider alternatives that may go with his changing role and recognize that an individual's decisions have effects on the actions of others.

A fine illustration of how this goal is developed in the minds of young twelfth-grade students is given in a description of a New York City class. The work centered around developing the "wheel of prosperity." This led to a consideration of profits and the use of such profits for the expansion of business which in turn, creates more jobs. An understanding of the interdependence of labor and capital was thus developed. The stake of the stockholder, the source of capital funds, union funds and employee investments, and government activity are areas of study which show the student how many different roles a citizen plays in the course of a day. These roles and decisions relevant to them may be conflicting ones and thus bring about a tempering of judgments. Alternative actions of each group in the economy are seen as interdependent and not unilateral.[11]

6. *A knowledge that economics as a discipline helps individuals*

9 Bureau of Business and Economic Research, *A Primer of Economics* (Series) (Iowa City: State University of Iowa).

10 *Level I—Economic Education* (Temple City, Calif.: Temple City Unified School District, 1963).

11 Ethel Garrison Cullen, "A Special Economics Course," *Economic Education Experiences of Enterprising Teachers, op. cit.,* pp. 1–11.

interpret phenomena and adjust to them in the light of personal and national interests. In the final analysis, the people make the decisions in the American society. The political structure of the country makes this possible. Responsibility is, therefore, judged through the due process of law. The "national interest" is no longer conceived as "laissez-faire" but is recognized as a desirable goal to be achieved. Desired results do not come from a policy of drifting in today's world. Public pressure and morality may serve as unwritten law, but abuse soon brings legal restriction. Gradually, a recognition has developed that accords to "national interest" an environment which makes for an improvement in self-interest.

> At Raleigh, North Carolina the ninth-grade students were helped to see this principle at work not as individuals yielding to national interests for their own sake, but as a nation yielding to world or Common Market interest.[12] Through the geography course, the problems of the European Economic Community countries were illustrated. Role playing enabled the students to demonstrate the disharmony before European Economic Community and the harmony which has occurred since its creation. The United States was used as an example. The states represented a free flow of resources and products, common currency, no traiff barriers and a location specialization that was very similar to the problems of the countries of Western Europe. It was a simple process to illustrate the displacement and the hardships that resulted with groups of people within a country because of the European Economic Community development, but measuring this against the aggregate gain for each nation brought insights that could easily be transferred to their own country. The concept of planning to achieve a growth pattern and a greater distribution of income for Western Europe, carried on by democratic countries, brought insights which would counteract the exhortations of the misinformed.

7. *A recognition that there are seldom any one-and-only "right" answers to the problems of economic life.* This is not to imply that the process of analysis and the tools that have been developed are not useful, but it is to point out that final economic decisions are made in the political realm and these often are influenced by tradition, morality, religion, and a number of other factors in one's environment. This accounts for the great stress on studying all of the alternatives and exercising "right of petition" in expressing prefer-

---

[12] C. Baxter Twiddy, "The European Economic Community," *Economic Education Experiences of Enterprising Teachers, op. cit.,* pp. 60–63.

ences. Each economic group is likely to perceive its own conclusion as the only "right" one but any one policy may be in conflict with other policies of other groups.

> Economics teaching lends itself to developing such a recognition. Through panels, personal interviews, debates, and brain teasers (fallacious statements), it is simple to get students to see how "logical" opposing points of view can be and how different people can have good reasons for different answers to problems. Economics does not always determine the course of action of a people. The Congress may request a lower budget but at the same time vote an increased expenditure for the "rivers and harbors" bill.
>
> Through a survey of local merchants it is possible for students to learn the various feelings and attitudes held by different persons in the same community and the reasons for them. Insights are gained on how different people solve problems in different ways.

Such, then, are the broad generalizations which economics as a discipline can develop through study. If economics can develop such understandings it will arm the student against propaganda, half-truths, emotional decisions, and rule by vested interests that are anxious to keep the public ignorant and susceptible to pat conclusions. Citizens must be able to distinguish between policies so that support may be given to that one which is in the national interest, for that is the one more nearly right.

Problem of grade placement.   The genius in teaching in the school program is in interpreting these broad generalizations into experiences for students at various grade levels. But it would be a mistake to assume that specific economic concepts can be isolated for study and treated exclusively at specific grade levels. If economics is considered to be a series of relationships, then these specific concepts must always be seen as part of an economic system. A study of one idea relationship immediately forces one into the adjacent idea and these quickly form a pattern. True, specific concepts or ideas may receive particular emphasis at particular grade levels, but never to the exclusion of the entire process and not in isolation from it.

Senesh, in his experiments with courses for children in the primary grades, has developed and adhered to what he has termed, *The Fundamental Idea Relationships of Economic Knowledge.*[13]

---

[13] Lawrence Senesh, *My Home, Curriculum Guide Social Studies Grade One* (Elkhart, Indiana: Elkhart Public Schools, 1960), p. 105.

Starting with the basic economic problem of unlimited wants and limited resources, the relationships are drawn to the immutable fact of specialization in its various forms creating the market to serve as a mediator to the conflict. The use of goods and services and the factors of production are determined by the market and the market decisions are modified by public policy which is based on the goals of American society. Any modification of the market system is the result of public policies.

Inherent in every classroom study and experience is the "total idea" relationship. The teacher must have clearly in mind the entire picture and must see how the particular area of discussion fits into the scheme of ideas. No matter at which grade economics is introduced the model remains the same. A greater depth and breadth are to be expected at each succeeding grade level.

At the primary level, where customarily the home is an important focal point, the concept of multiple wants and limited resources can be taught through a simple listing and recital of family wants and resources represented by family income. Within the family, division of labor (specialization) can be examined for efficiency. Interdependence follows from this and the understanding is made clear that while some family members are both producers and consumers others are merely consumers. Discussions on occupational desires, or job preferences help introduce the role of the market as a decision-maker. Here the factors of production can be clearly seen in the determination of jobs and, by the same token, loss of employment can be demonstrated. Developing the national picture on aggregate family demand is possible here, and it follows that family decisions are thus related to the social goals of society. The idea relationships are evident.[14]

In the intermediate grades, the pupil is introduced to peoples and cultures in other parts of the nation. At the Fort Dodge, Iowa, Schools, "The Changing South" is investigated at the fifth-grade level.[15] A reading of a story by Lois Lenski entitled *Strawberry Girl* gave the project the needed emphasis. Tradition, the movement of labor to more productive occupations through the market, the

---

[14] Lawrence Senesh, *The World at Work, Working and Earning* (Lafayette, Indiana: Purdue Research Foundation, 1963).

[15] Mildred Alexander and Ingeborg Highland, "Economic Education in the Intermediate Grades," *Educating for Economic Competence* (Washington, D.C.: Association for Supervision and Curriculum Development, 1960), pp. 40–48.

interaction of work and consumer demands, the importance of capital and natural resources, and understandings developed in connection with economic growth, were illustrated with this story. History, through the illustration of the tobacco trade, brought out consumer demand, specialization, and multilateral trade. Technological improvement was illustrated by the invention of the cotton gin, and the relationship was drawn between such inventions and productivity increases and the market and price structures. Choice of crops to be raised by the farmer was shown to be based on potential profit. Later on, the natural resources of the South were studied as a basis for the new industrial potential of that part of the country. Comparative advantage as a concept was developed from a comparison of products of the South with those of Iowa.

A junior high school in New York, operating in an environment entirely different from Fort Dodge, undertook a study of America's resource problem.[16] Their interest grew out of a historical study of America's industrial development and its counterpart, the technological revolution. This led to a concern for the rapidity with which resources were being used up. Initiating activities led to posing a problem of the relationship of resources and their use in achieving a higher standard of living. In addition to a study of the resource base today, a look to the future was provided through a study reported by Resources for the Future, Inc.[17] Alternative uses of resources were considered and alternative resources for the same use were considered in relationship to cost. Controls on the production of natural resources were examined and alternative policies scrutinized. Comparative costs, effects of new technology, effects of labor efficiency and use in light of the development of more efficient resources, and lack of labor mobility and capital investment in the coal industry were seen as parts of the idea relationship of the market and price system.

Rapid community growth was the subject of a study by an eleventh-grade group of students in a suburb of Los Angeles.[18] Rates of change in population, housing, number of automobiles,

---

[16] Edythe Gaines, "Economic Education in the Junior High School," *Educating for Economic Competence, op. cit.,* pp. 49–58.

[17] *The Nation Looks At Its Resources* (Washington, D.C.: Resources For The Future, Inc., 1954).

[18] Frances Hall Adams, "Economic Education in the Senior High School," *Educating for Economic Competence, op. cit.,* pp. 59–67.

THE FUNDAMENTAL IDEA RELATIONSHIPS OF ECONOMIC KNOWLEDGE

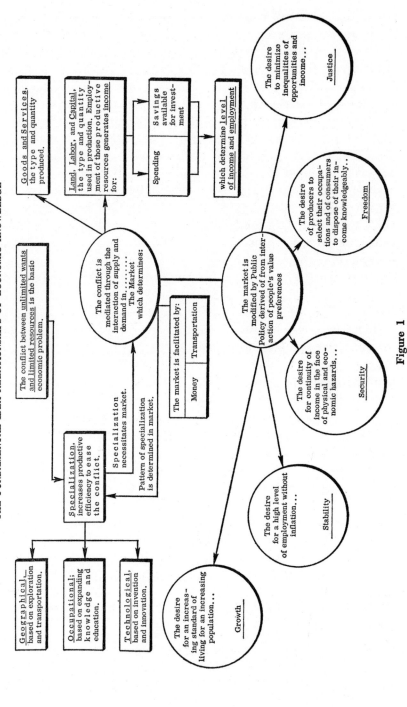

Figure 1

retail sales, occupational structure, employment, bank deposits and the like, were studied. The growth of Los Angeles was compared to the growth in other sections of the nation, and the decline in some areas was checked as well. The factors of production were seen in light of availability and mobility. Growth was analyzed and subsequently recognized as being something other than progress. There were costs involved in population growth, and the utilization of land was seen through a study of industry, housing, or recreation. Similarly, the water problem, transportation, and the increase in government expenditures and services, were other problems for investigation. All of these had a relationship to the tax structure. Sociological as well as political factors had to be taken into account. Such a study brought the students face to face with the problem of economic scarcity, productivity, resource allocation, comparative advantage, marginal utility, opportunity costs, economic multiplier, Gross National Product, income flow and production of goods and services, economic costs versus social costs, and cyclical growth patterns.

These four descriptions of class projects can be superimposed on the *Fundamental Idea Relationship* chart (Fig. 1) developed by Senesh.[19] Note the concern in each project with the allocation problem, the market and price system, specialization, utilization of resources, the development of public policy, and the relationship of these to the social goals. Each classroom study projected a greater degree of sophistication and the experiences provided the student were compatible with his vocabulary level and his maturity. The experiences were rooted in a familiar environment, but the expansion of this environment to encompass the national scene was also in evidence.

Economics can then be seen as a unity at any grade level, not as a fractured study. Theory is developed through the experiences provided by the school that have relevance to the life of the student. There was no need to belabor the point of "economics for what?" The application of economic reasoning and theory to realistic situations characterized each one of the projects and thus a motivation for study was present.

---

[19] Senesh, *My Home, Curriculum Guide Social Studies Grade One, op. cit.,* p. 105.

CHAPTER III

Developing a School Program

Since 1948, the Joint Council on Economic Education and its state and regional affiliates have been assisting schools throughout the nation in developing more adequate programs of economic education. Schools, however, have been doing some work in this area for many years, and economic understanding has been a cited objective of education in the American schools. Scarcely a school system did not have economic education as one of its goals. Only recently, however, has there been widespread concern to give this area of learning a higher priority than it had previously. In creating this acceptance of emphasis on economic education in the curriculum, the Joint Council has played the major role as organizer, stimulater, coordinator and experimenter.

During its history, the Joint Council has profited by the many experiences it has had in schools, colleges, and communities. Trial and error leading to success, which is so typical of the social sciences, has brought about an understanding of the problems to be faced in developing a school program. Looking at these problems is the first step in developing ways of overcoming them.

Problems

1. *To the average person the word "economics" connotes controversy, an argument, a difference of opinion.* Reading the newspapers, listening to a political debate or a television discussion reveals to many people the controversial nature of economics. This is the first problem in developing a school program. Economics, as a discipline, is applied to issues in public and private sectors and issues are always controversial.

2. *The schools are often the victims of partisan policies designed to persuade rather than educate.* In the course of any given year, several hundred pamphlets and other materials are contributed to the schools by various organizations and deposited on the teacher's

31

desk. Hundreds of interest groups in business, industry, labor, agriculture, trade associations, patriotic organizations, government, and foundations, let alone publishers, are engaged in producing materials concerned with propagating a particular policy point of view, and the captive audience in the schools is looked upon as fair game for the consumption of such policy statements. How many of them are adequate for the classroom can be seen from the experiences of the Materials Evaluation Committee which in its first report selected but 97 items from among the 7,000 reviewed.[1] In the second report, only 65 were selected from among 4,000 reviewed. Attempts are being made to utilize the schools to indoctrinate the student in believing a particular course of action or brand of economic philosophy. But this is not to be wholly decried, for "the right of petition" is one that guarantees to all citizens the right to be heard. The responsibility for the use of such material, however, lies with the teacher in developing the competency to guide the student to more discerning and analytical judgments in this search for greater economic sophistication.

3. *The inadequate preparation of the teachers in economics and the consequent lack of the very understanding they are trying to impart to their pupils is another of the major problems in developing a sound school program.* Many claim that the reason teachers avoid economics in their own preparation is because the subject has been poorly presented. Others claim that the methods used and the selection of content offered have been dry, useless, difficult, and abstract. Whether correct or not, these impressions are prevalent among teachers, and they are shared by many of the certification authorities in state departments of education. In only 22 states in this country is any formal background in economics a requirement for the teaching of social studies, let alone for general teacher background.[2]

The National Task Force on Economic Education, in surveying the background in economics of social studies teachers, found them either woefully deficient in their preparation in economics or else the preparation was of such a vintage that there was a relatively minor relationship to economics of the latter half of the twentieth

---

[1] *Study Materials for Economic Education in the Schools,* Report of the Materials Evaluation Committee, Supplementary Paper No. 12 (New York: Committee for Economic Development, October, 1961).

[2] *A Survey of States' Teacher Certification Requirements* (New York: Joint Council on Economic Education, 1963).

century.[3] In the first report of the National Task Force, a minimum of six semester hours is recommended for all social studies and business education teachers with an additional year's preparation cited as desirable. For those teaching a separate course in economics at the high school level, a minor (18 semester hours) was recommended. Certification authorities in the states have not faced up to the educational requirements needed to produce an adequately trained social studies teacher in today's world. A background in history, with little or no concentration in the other social sciences, is still acceptable. And so an outmoded pattern continues to be fostered.

Teachers do not want to teach what they do not know. Even when the curriculum calls for economics, it would be well to see how it is being taught in the classroom. Such examination of the curriculum probably will show that due to tradition the social studies curriculum, in which economics and the other social sciences are equal participants, is history-oriented. To justify this in today's world would be difficult, especially since the great majority of youth (approximately two-thirds) do not go beyond the high school in their formal education. The very definition of social studies implies offerings in all of the various disciplines that constitute the field. To seek to achieve a better balance of emphasis is not easy, for it requires disengaging vested interests and combating inertia. In part, the study of history has achieved this prominence because of political pressure groups or patriotic groups that have made their weight felt. There is some confusion over what kind of knowledge instills patriotism, but history has had the most vociferous supporters. Such pressures have not appeared in support of economics, but this is not to say that the tenor of the times will not produce such activity.

Couple these specific problems related to the teaching of economics with the general problems faced by the schools in any curriculum revision, and the challenge of economic education becomes of even greater magnitude. Teacher apathy is present within the schools to the same degree that it exists in any other profession. Teachers are not always anxious to overcome a deficiency in substantive and methodological background. Besides, teachers are sub-

---

[3] *Economic Education in the Schools*, Report of the National Task Force on Economic Education (New York: Committee for Economic Development, September, 1961).

jected to so many pressures to devote more time to other subjects or areas that extra efforts or changes are avoided.

Today's world requires, however, that there be a continual effort to update and upgrade teacher education. Rigid college standards, prescribed for in-service programs, are so little related to the needs of both teachers and the curriculum that the tendency of public school systems is to avoid college-sponsored programs. Teachers, oftentimes, see little relationship between what the courses contain, either by example of instruction or content, and what would help them do a more effective job in the classroom. The present tendency to draw a dichotomy between the content and the method or to disregard method as an integral part of effective teaching by government sponsored programs is a step backward and one that is far removed from reality. The inclination of those in the profession to seek a scapegoat for that which they themselves have created is inexcusable.

4. *School systems are unable to budget funds for in-service education or provide released teacher time for curriculum development.* School systems face the problem, just as industry does, of being forced to plan and operate in-service or preparation programs at their own expense. Board of education members, many of whom are making daily decisions in their own companies for continual expansion of their research and development efforts and for personnel policies to improve the efficiency of their operations, see little relationship between these decisions and those they make as board members. Education is not yet viewed as capital investment in this society and schools suffer because of the inability of school boards to understand the economics of education.

5. *A major problem that has to be faced by all who are concerned with education is the one of the competence of its educational leadership.* Here the situation is similar to that of any other profession or occupation in the country. But perhaps education can be accused of not, itself, setting its administrative standards high enough to bring the competencies desired. Too often the attitude is one of "not rocking the boat," and without strong leadership, developing curriculum becomes a "laissez-faire" proposition resulting in aimless wandering.

6. *Curriculum planning has suffered from the failure of schools to establish priorities.* Objectives are beautifully detailed in state-

ment after statement for the educational program but, strangely enough, there is a wide gulf between the basic interests of today's world and tomorrow's needs and the objectives stated. The question, "Changes for what?" has not been answered. Events such as the first sputnik caused untold pressures on the schools and so education proceeded to go off on a scientific "binge" which so affected the curriculum that it is still trying to regain its equilibrium. Fear, pressures, and critics who desire us to emulate school programs of other countries with different societal goals have prevented the professionally prepared planners from settling down. The leadership that is in the schools has been abrogated, and the concept of American schools serving to educate the children of all the people of the community has been circumscribed to mean in too many cases, "serving to educate the children of all the people of the community to accept the decisions of a special interest group."

7. *And finally, problems in curriculum change are to be found in the textbooks, school curriculum guides, teaching units, and vested interests within the faculty itself.* Certainly schools need to look at research and development programs just as industry and government do. Where revision is required because the evidence indicates a deficiency in this area then revision must occur. The length of time a textbook remains in use in a school system should not depend on its cost; but unfortunately, where curriculum is wedded to the text, it does. "Teachers' Guides" and units cannot be looked upon as permanent, but as items which may have to undergo model changes each year. Justice Douglas defined the problem succinctly when he stated: "Many public school textbooks have been so watered down to meet the objections of the most conventional-minded member of the school board that they are incredibly dull. The whole excitement and challenge of modern economic and political issues are lost. Is this the kind of education we want?"[4]

These, then, are the problems which the Joint Council on Economic Education has encountered in its work with schools across the country. But these are generalizations not to be found in entirety in every school system although degrees of each can be found there. A set of sound principles of operation has evolved in developing a program of economic education. Experiences of the Joint Council

---

4 William O. Douglas, *A Living Bill of Rights* (New York: Doubleday & Company, Inc., 1961), p. 67.

with a series of cooperating school systems, countless demonstration projects, teacher-preparation programs, materials development and community organization, have provided the matrix from which these conclusions were drawn. The environment within which they were developed is as diversified as the United States, but the common characteristics are universal in their application.

Solutions to the Problems

1. *Increasing the economic understanding of teachers.* Evolution generates much more confidence than revolution. No creative thinking in curriculum revision will occur until the teachers and administrators feel at home in their knowledge of economics. Since there is this lack of economic understanding among most educators in community schools, and even more so on the part of the body politic as a whole, the approach should start from where the people are.

Every summer there are many workshops and institutes on economic education held at universities and colleges throughout the country. Developing economic education leaders in the schools, creating an awareness of the materials and other resources available for program development, establishing relationships between the economist, educator, and community are all features of the Joint Council program that has so successfully stimulated enthusiasm in the teaching profession. Here the participants gain a basic understanding of what economics is all about and develop plans for interpreting this knowledge for their pupils. However, even when this is accomplished, action on a school-wide basis must await decisions by the administration and the school board.

The next logical step is to get many teachers from the same school system involved either in summer programs or programs held during the school year. Possibilities exist to develop programs to meet the specific needs of a school and community. Experiences can be provided for teachers similar to those which the teachers can provide for the students. By meeting with fellow teachers from all grades, each is permitted to see his own work in relation to the total program, Grades one through twelve. Leadership in developing programs, institutional plans, and materials is in the hands of the teacher at the local level where it is most effective. The choice of what to

period [brought about a change in] the American people's attitude . . . toward the government's role in the economy."[8]

Economic analysis applied to history brings a consideration of political science and sociology along with it. Through these new dimensions in the history course, intellectual curiosity is developed. Events
of the past do not become terminal but germinal, triggering reactions
which may be explosive in character.

Such experimentation leads to course revision. But evolution has
been the method of procedure. Throughout, the teacher is involved
in the planning and development of such programs in order that the
special needs of his own community and its youth may be met. As
more teachers become involved, more experimentation takes place.
The teachers who participate in such programs work with experts
both in economics and curriculum development. The leaders in the
community are also involved in the process, thus minimizing fears
that may exist of domination by those in the community whose attitude is, "MY policy is the only right one."

The kindergarten through twelfth-grade program, even though it
may be more difficult and longer, is the only approach that will insure economic literacy at the end of the school experience. Economics as a study cuts across course lines in the schools; it is a
thread of understanding which begins to be woven through the early
experiences of a child and strengthens itself through a series of experiences as each year of his life passes. The elementary school presents the simpler problem since the unit of study deals with the
entire life of the student, and he is expected to shift gears at the
end of each class hour. Successful approaches will involve a development of skills on a spiral with an ever-increasing complexity and
difficulty adjusted to the maturity of the learner. One impression
that has been gained is that no technique or method is too difficult
if adjusted to the experiences of the student.

4. *Learning proceeds best when it operates in an environment
with which the student is familiar.* For instance, in one senior class
the problem of conservation and resource-use was studied. The relationships of this one problem to the entire community were
developed by the teacher.

Take, as a larger example, the "Problems of American Democ-

---

[8] Senesh, "Social Goals of The Economy," *Educating for Economic Competence,
op. cit.,* p. 18.

use, with whom, and when can only be made at this level, even though the experts have provided the items to choose from. Special conferences, seminars, and selected lectures tend to keep the teacher abreast of new knowledge on a continuing basis. The vast majority of these programs are jointly sponsored by collegiate institutions, and teachers are offered degree credits for their successful fulfillment. Strengthening the school-university tie is a necessary ingredient to success.

In essence, teacher competency in economic education is necessary for discerning judgments and for proper guidance for students in achieving economic understanding. The first step in the creation of a culture is to develop within the student a consciousness of the potentials of his present environment and intelligent insights into the significance of these potentials for building a better future.

It was to this very assignment that the National Task Force on Economic Education addressed itself. A framework of the minimum understanding in economics necessary for effective citizenship and the world of work was developed by the Task Force to provide over-all guidelines for a twelve-year school program.

> The case for economic understanding [is not] limited to preparation for effective voting. Leaders in every walk of life . . . need to understand the American economy, as do the people who work for the businesses and who are members of the union. . . . We can act rationally [perception] that is, on the basis of a reasonable understanding of how the economy operates, a clear recognition of the goals we want to achieve, an appraisal of relevant facts, and a reasoned choice of that line of action which will best achieve our goals . . . the primary obligation of the schools is to help the student develop the capacity to think clearly, objectively, and with a reasonable degree of sophistication about economic problems.[5]

The assignment is to get the present and future teachers prepared to take on this responsibility.

2. *There is a recognition that most of what is now being taught in our schools offers opportunities to develop economic understanding.* A new dimension is being added to the regular classroom units, a dimension that leads from the descriptive to the analytical. Emphasis is placed on improving the ability of the teacher to utilize the tools of economic analysis for achieving proficiency in solving economic problems.

---

[5] *Economic Education in the Schools, op. cit.,* pp. 8, 13.

racy" course, which traces through teaching units the roles of markets, skills and technological relationships, purchasing power, personal efficiency and, finally, the relation of market decisions to the flow of goods and services and the flow of income.[9] Initiating the study with the personal interests of the student, analysis is gradually introduced at three levels of comprehension which enables the student to see first his own job, then the labor market, and, finally, the American economic system as a continuous, unfolding unit.

The community becomes a laboratory in which the socioeconomic problems of the nation and the world are studied and analyzed. At one time in the history of this country, every youngster became familiar with the economic life of his community by simply walking down Main Street. Today, however, most youth are strangers in their own communities; yet these communities contain all of the ingredients for broad economic study. This accounts for the emphasis on programs that are local in character.

What is true of the pupil is true of the teacher as well. A study of community resources becomes an integral part of an economic education program for both. Resource persons serve as consultants. Field trips related to the classroom work in progress are utilized. Files are developed on the "who" and "what" in the community.

Workshops also lend assistance. Time is spent discussing the economy of the state or region. Studies conducted by state industrial development commissions and research bureaus become significant when the program starts with a recognizable focus. Publications such as "Kalamazoo Today,"[10] "The Akron Story,"[11] and "Greater Hartford . . . A Helicopter View"[12] are examples of what results when teachers have been stimulated to meet the needs of their students for good material. And more of this will be done throughout the school systems of our country.

Schools must recognize that the curriculum in the social studies cannot be wedded to the text. Teachers, parents, and other members of the community must establish whether the text is *the answer* or simply *one tool* to be used to create understanding. Sufficient experi-

---

[9] *Problems of Democracy, Supplement to the Course of Study #126* (Akron: Akron Public Schools, 1956).

[10] *Kalamazoo Today* (Kalamazoo: Kalamazoo Public Schools, 1955).

[11] *The Akron Story* (Akron: The Board of Education of Akron, 1959).

[12] *Greater Hartford . . . A Helicopter View* (Hartford: Greater Hartford Council on Economic Education, 1958).

mentation has taken place to indicate that there is no simple pattern of learning for all students. The written material, the visual and audio aids, the text and the pamphlets, the newspaper and magazine, the TV, movies, bulletin board displays, recordings, and actual conversations with the informed must be integrated to be beneficial to young people from different backgrounds and with different abilities.

When teachers have latitude in the selection of materials, a situation is established which allows for creative expression on the part of both teacher and class. In such an environment, the underachievers can find a sense of satisfaction and school takes on a new meaning. Such treatment to the process of learning reflects itself in a diversified class organization and permits a wide variation in achievement and interest.

The goal of successful pupil achievement is gained by sacrificing breadth in factual information for depth in analytical treatment. The teacher of the social studies may want pupils to acquire an understanding of society and also may want them to memorize a great deal of factual content. These two ends are inconsistent. The feeling persists that the textbook must be covered, and often "digging in" is sacrificed in order to get through the text. For instance, the teacher may recognize that the J. P. Morgan incident in profiting on government bonds to avoid a serious depression during the 1890's is a perfect spot to study the ups and downs of business and the economy. But because there are still three to four hundred pages to cover in the textbook, he does not take time for the examination of business cycles and continues on to the next page. Teaching understanding is time-consuming, but taking time to think about some of the contents pays dividends for the student. The contents of a textbook can only be learned by "rote memorization," but meaning is developed by experiences. It is here that the teacher and school must make choices between conceptual and associationist learning.

5. *The cooperation and sponsorship of many groups in the economy will insure the success of a school-wide effort.* True enough, experiences in the classroom are dependent upon the cooperation of public school administrators and devoted and interested teachers. But more is needed. A joint approach by school, university, and community is required. The universities have gained a great deal. Contact with the schools has given professors the experience of the face-to-face reality of the classroom needed to improve what they

were doing in their own classes. Universities possess the resources that are of major assistance in producing a better equipped and confident teacher. Professors of economics are being used extensively to consult with teachers. Many institutions have reorganized or instituted courses in economics for the future teacher that are functional and that provide a foundation for future work assignments in the classroom. Materials are produced that answer the needs. This is the kind of relationship among all the participants in the program that can make the teaching of economics a dynamic and vital part of the school curriculum.

Throughout the country, economists are being enlisted in the struggle against economic illiteracy, and the profession as a whole is gearing itself to meet the challenge. It is foolish to think of economic education without the economist. He can help to develop an informed teacher who can face with equanimity the multitude of pressures which come from special interest groups.

The community also has a role in economic education. In every instance where the Joint Council has assisted, community advisory groups on economic education have been organized. Today there is a network of 41 state and regional councils, affiliated with the Joint Council, yet autonomously and independently carrying on this work. In every instance business, labor, and agricultural leaders have joined the educators in the program. Through their efforts, resources and consultants are made available for various projects. In this way, teachers and professors are brought together in a healthy working relationship with leading citizens in the community, and thus mutual respect is engendered.

Community interest at this level is an important stimulant for action. Teacher confidence is developed. A sense of belonging to the community is created. Valuable resources are placed at the disposal of the schools. Doors that once seemed closed are suddenly opened. A strong core of influential citizens materializes to accept the responsibility of lending personal assistance. Support for the teacher and the school is provided by a representative lay-citizen group so that curriculum development and teaching improvement can take place in an atmosphere of security. The school is taken out of the arena of indoctrination and permitted to emphasize true education in its finest sense.

Economic education, as stated previously, cannot be equated

with education in any of the other disciplines. Since 1948, the Joint Council on Economic Education, through its basic philosophy, method of operation, its adherence to educational precepts, and respect for educational leadership, has developed a reputation for integrity. Educators, economists, and many national organizations have been alerted to the need for improving economic literacy and now work with the Joint Council to satisfy this need. Excellent working arrangements also have been developed with other economic education organizations, notably the Family Finance Program and the Council for the Advancement of Secondary Education. Two fine reports, *Economic Literacy for Americans*,[13] and *How To Plan Economic Understanding Projects*[14] are available. The AFL-CIO has demonstrated its belief in the program in published letters to its constituents from its president, George Meany. Major research, business, labor and agricultural organizations are lending their support throughout the country. Many of the leading divisions of the National Education Association maintain a direct affiliation with the Joint Council. Financial sponsorship has come from major foundations and the various groups mentioned above. Great strength and confidence in the program were added several years ago by the direct affiliation of the American Economic Association to the Joint Council, a unique distinction.

An environment for good economic education had to be created and this has been accomplished. Confidence in the schools has been generated and the community has slowly been convinced, not only of the need, but of the desirability of the program.

There cannot be any overnight miracles in curriculum change in economics. The reasons have been outlined above. Change will not occur by a flick of a switch or by a formula. Above all, change depends on the teacher. Many misconceptions and prejudices have to be replaced by reasoned analysis. But the tools for a successful program leading to an analytical approach in the schools have been developed and are listed below:

1. The report of the National Task Force, *Economic Education in the Schools,* prepared by a distinguished group of economists and educators

---

[13] *Economic Literacy for Americans* (New York: Committee for Economic Development, 1962).

[14] *How To Plan Economic Understanding Projects* (Washington, D.C.: Chamber of Commerce of the United States, 1963).

appointed by the American Economic Association.[15] In the report the basic framework of the minimum understanding of economics for high school students has been defined.

2. Publication of the two reports, *Study Materials for Economic Education in the Schools,* prepared by an outstanding group of experts charged with the responsibility for selecting materials suitable as supplementary readings in economics by high school students.[16]

3. Production of a national college-credit television course, "The American Economy," providing a means of improving teacher background and classroom practice.[17] Kinescopes of the program sessions are available for continued use.

4. Construction of tests for diagnostic purposes in evaluating school programs by the Commission for Measurement of Economic Understanding.[18]

5. Availability of teaching materials. Increasingly, publishers are offering a variety of materials in economics. Well-developed publications, recordings, filmstrips, films, and charts are available for student use. Supplementary materials to the text are also becoming increasingly popular. Similarly many materials to assist the teacher are obtainable for all grade levels and courses.

---

[15] *Economic Education in the Schools, op. cit.*

[16] *Study Materials for Economic Education in the Schools, op. cit.*

[17] "The American Economy," *op. cit.*

[18] Commission for Measurement of Economic Understanding, *Test of Economic Understanding* (Chicago: Science Research Associates, 1963).

CHAPTER IV

Basic Assumption in Curriculum Development in Economic Education

The public school systems have long accepted economic education as a major objective for the curriculum. A review of the teachers' guides, courses of study, and philosophic underpinnings of published school reports indicates that the goals of economic citizenship and economic proficiency were emphasized. The gap between "what is" and "what should be" was large, however, especially in light of the new era the world had moved into. Conditions demanded a higher priority for an analytical approach to economics.

Good curriculum practice in the schools is applicable in any area, but there is direct relevance of this to economics. Added support for a K–12 program in economic education becomes evident from an examination of the basic assumptions discussed below.

1. *Attention must be given to establishing a broader curriculum which is designed to meet the needs and interests of both society and the pupils who are developing into mature members of that society.* If the question is raised as to the most important understandings necessary for citizenship and for a productive life the answer will be found in two areas—an understanding of our democracy, the way it functions, its obligations and guarantees, and an understanding of our economic system. These are the foundation stones upon which the American society rests. Such basic understanding is vital if our way of life is to continue.

The curriculum of the schools must reflect the purposes of the society for which it exists. The commitment to an economic education program becomes evident.

2. *The curriculum should be related to factual situations and experiences.* As John Dewey said, "We *use* our past experiences to construct new and better ones in the future. The very fact of experience thus includes the process by which it directs itself in its own

betterment."[1] The direction of personality development is determined largely by the social environment within which the child interacts. It is common knowledge that the infant's only chance to grow into a human being is through his social relationships. A personality can develop only through the social contacts it has with its fellow men. Society is the medium through which its members become human. All persons exist because the environment makes it possible for them to do so. A democratic society provides the greatest opportunity for human development. Individualism, then, is given its greatest impetus. A premium is placed on the respect of one for another. Security is provided by this mutual respect. People are encouraged to use their initiative and creative talents by the groups of which they are members. Personalities are enriched through learning to live and to cooperate with others who make up the society.

To illustrate: A study of the Scandinavian countries was made by a class in an elementary school in Washington. The aim was to give the students an appreciation of the culture of those countries and the contributions they made culturally and economically to the United States. The Scandinavian parentage of many of the children, plus the proximity to a fishing community made up mainly of Scandinavian immigrants provided an excellent focus. A study of the geographical conditions and their relationship to the economic life of both areas, the problems that had to be met, and the industries developed, led to appreciation of cultural differences. The utilization of material resources, the effect of climate, and means of transportation were compared to those of the United States. Energy was seen as a component factor in economic development. Multilateral trade was easily illustrated. The initiative and creative talents of people were viewed in light of the industries developed. The project was woven around the immediate environment of the pupils, but through the use of maps, films, and a series of books the students were led to broader horizons.

3. *Curriculum development programs should start with the student.* Recognizing that in our society today there is a wide variety of interests, it should be expected that the students in any given classroom will reflect a diversity of background and development.

---

[1] John Dewey, *Reconstruction in Philosophy* (Boston: Beacon Press, Inc., 1948), p. 95.

School programs, therefore, must attempt to meet individual differences. This may be done by starting with the student. A variety of teaching materials and procedures must be utilized too, if this is to be accomplished.

Varied teaching materials are beginning to make their appearance. Charts are now available from publishers. Pamphlets, both as text materials and for supplementary use, are also at hand. Textbooks for high school economics courses are plentiful. Films and filmstrips have been especially prepared for both the elementary and secondary schools. There is still much to be done, however, for those areas of economics left untouched, and the grade sequence of materials leaves much to be desired.

Insufficient attention has been given to developing procedures and programs for work with the less able students. Akron, New York City, and Detroit are school systems where ninth-grade programs have been instituted to meet this need. Tulsa, Oklahoma, offers a well-developed program for its eighth-grade students, and there are many other notable examples throughout the country.

Methodological approaches in great variety have also made an appearance. Many examples are found in *Economic Topics,* the "how to teach" articles.[2] The Newton, Masachusetts school system has developed a number of case studies for economic education, and Duluth has had successful experiences at the senior level of the secondary school with the use of "The American Economy" TV series.[3] The project method, on an individual and committee basis, may be seen in Scott High School, East Orange, New Jersey. Common to all these experiences seems to be the avoidance of the lecture or the simple question-answer techniques.

4. *Effecting improvement in any school program means considering the use of pupil interest as a motivating factor of learning.* As the student moves from grades one through twelve and then to college, the use of pupil interest as a motivation varies in inverse ratio. Rather than raising the question of what kind of things are important for the teacher to teach, economics, as a discipline, lends itself to a question related to proper motivation. If a start is made with the

---

[2] *Economic Topics* (New York: Joint Council on Economic Education). This publication has appeared three times a year for the past five years. It is a continuing project of the Joint Council's program.

[3] "The American Economy," *op. cit.,* p. 71.

questions that ask what kind of problems are important to young-sters going through the school program and how pupils can learn to deal with these problems more effectively, then economics can con-tribute to a better understanding of these problems. It does not detract from the discipline, but puts it to work in a different frame of reference.

The search for the ideas, processes, concepts, or problems that should be taught at a given age is a waste of time. The truth is that any concept can be taught to any child at any age if it is done within the scope of his experience, in words and situations that he under-stands and that challenge him.

5. *Emphasis should be placed on correlating and integrating areas of learning.* Education today has a responsibility to provide some synthesis for the learner. Compartmentalization should be relegated to a secondary role and an emphasis on the interrelation-ships between areas of learning be substituted in order that the knowledge becomes meaningful to the learner. Curriculum planners should be constantly building into classwork a sensitivity to the relations between the simple, personal, day-to-day kinds of situa-tions and problems and those broad, very serious, very important social issues which affect the whole of society and not simply the individual.

In education, many people are trying to develop the kinds of materials which are adaptable for use all through the school cur-riculum, in various stages of chronological development, and in the broad subject-area fields. As the professional approaches the prob-lems which are of broad concern to people, one finds that the tools used in solving these problems are of importance in many areas of the school curriculum, since materials produced can be made adapt-able to a variety of subject areas.

Until the broad social issues are related to personal and com-munity problems, what is produced will be partial and ineffective. If the personal problems are ignored, what will be developed will be a kind of abstract and overly academic approach to economics which is based on a faulty psychology and which does not represent the interrelationship of the factors within the discipline itself. If one remains only with the personal and consumer aspects of economics, however, there will be a failure to create the understandings that will help young people bridge the gap between personal problems and the broad continuing social issues.

6. *Curriculum development today puts a premium on cooperative planning by students and teachers.* If the assumption is accepted that education is a process that increases the ability of a person to become self-directed, then the premise must be accepted. Remembering also that the goal is educating for a democracy, developing the initiative of each person to its fullest degree is the goal for which all schools should strive. All that has been said emphasizes that the greatest advances are made through a program based on the "needs and interests" of the student. Obviously, this approach can be achieved only by a pupil-teacher relationship of mutual respect and understanding.

"Needs and interests" is often a misunderstood phrase. It does not mean a concern for the student's immediate, expressed surface problem alone. It does not mean a discussion of this problem followed by some superficial investigation, reporting the results of this superficiality, and then considering the problem solved. Rather, it begins with the need as a motivating factor and moves out from horizon to horizon, in ever-widening circles, taking the young people beyond their immediate interest point to dealing with elementary basic concepts. (The student's immediate interest can be likened to a pebble dropped into the water, and the circles created as the ever-widening area of his concern.)

In other words, it is important to capitalize on their initial enthusiasm and, by this means, to develop a desire to study in a penetrating fashion. Answering student questions as posed might result in a simple answer. But real education results when students are taken on the road leading to deeper significance, eventually arriving at the point where action is required. Each teacher must plot with the students the significant learnings that are involved and determine the larger goals involved originally in the simple question; then proceed to guide the activities to enable the goals to be reached.

The potential of developing self-direction rests here. Each pupil as he plans can project himself into the future, establish goals he hopes to achieve, and select from his environment those situations and experiences which will enable him to reach his goals. He can build upon his past experiences and evaluate the new in light of these. He is, in fact, constantly building his own environment. This requires an understanding of the problem, a weighing of the results of alternative courses of action, and a selection of those experiences which will contribute to greater self-realization.

The Akron, Ohio, Schools, in their revision of the "Problems of Democracy" course to include an emphasis on economics, starts from the interest of the student in his future occupation.[4] Three units of work are developed and arranged so that the student is brought along from a consideration of his own chances for a job to a broader look at some problems of labor and management, and, finally, to see that the market situation presented to him in the other units can be generalized to show some of the important aspects of the kind of system in which he lives. The teacher is given the responsibility of tracing through three units: (1) the interest of the student in his vocational problems, (2) the role of markets, the student's skills and technology, his purchasing power, personal efficiency, and (3) the relation of market decisions to the flow of goods and services and the flow of income. This arrangement thus combines the resource units in such a way as to satisfy both the demands of education with regard to increasingly abstract economic relations.

7. *Curriculum development demands that the school and community cooperate in the process.* Most citizens have a real interest in the schools which educate their children and supply the community with its employees and market. Civic pride and responsibility also create a positive attitude in meeting any request which comes from the schools. Students, teachers, and the community can plan together for the most effective type of learning experiences.

When the curriculum is defined as inclusive of all the influences within the responsibility of the school that affect the development of the students, the task of organizing a program of education is seen in a new perspective. Economics, by its very nature, is ideally suited for such a relationship. The interest in economics is already high in the community, and the subject matter is of such importance that the community groups feel impelled to be in on the programming for what they deem to be their own benefit. The school is in the unique position of capitalizing on this interest and turning what may seem to be a selfish motive into positive group participation.

8. *Use of community resources is essential in economic education.* These resources may be defined as those which may be brought

---

[4] *Problems of Democracy, Supplement to the Course of Study #126, op. cit.*

into the classroom and those which the students use in the community itself, often outside the school, even though for certain purposes the school and the classroom become the "community." Community resources are not completely isolated from the home, the school, the classroom, and the students because these areas are continually interacting with each other. All of these influences are operating to provide an environment which affects the student.

If the definition of the curriculum presented above is followed, undoubtedly, such a curriculum must utilize community resources because of the great opportunity to affect the development of the student and make economic theory a reality. The student achieves satisfaction through using the community in seeking solutions to problems, because his own social development is advanced, and, at the same time, he is increasing his understanding in a content area. The opportunity to make content more meaningful by utilizing actual situations in the community provides a base for curriculum construction in economics and teacher reeducation which is in line with the research findings on how children learn. Perhaps the most important technique in the learning process is the contrived experience, in this instance, selected, organized, and completed by the student.

Economic education should not be bound by the school walls. Written material is necessary to acquire understanding, but this does not suffice to create the realism that is inherent in the study. Knowledge can be understood better if it is actively sought. Each community is a microcosmic society illustrating a realistic operation of the theoretical model. "Factories and farms, stores and governing agencies, unions and trade associations, business, labor and government leaders . . . these, as well as books, films, and other 'school' helps to learning are the basic materials out of which the modern school's educational program is built."[5]

The Teachers Guide To The Use of Community Resources in Economic Education details the multiple resources which exist in the community for use in economic education and provides a number of actual illustrations of classroom projects utilizing such resources successfully.[6]

---

[5] *Teachers Guide To The Use of Community Resources in Economic Education* (New York: Joint Council on Economic Education, 1955), p. 12.
[6] *Ibid.*

9. *Educators are coming to realize that energy and time can be saved by organizing instruction around larger units and relating these units to over-all problems.* Increasing specialization has fragmented the curriculum. Students are hard put to recognize the interrelationship of the discipline areas. Skills are taught, too often, as isolated bits of training and not as tools necessary for achieving an understanding of pertinent problems. Norman Cousins states this so well when he considers the question of what education is expected to do.[7] According to Cousins, education is responsible for developing the science of interrelationship, thereby producing an integration of knowledge to create meaning. Students are not gaining insights into the meaning and purpose of education itself. Little effort is made to provide "direction and destination" for the isolated and compartmentalized approach which education is today. Students must observe the interaction of events and ideas. The problems which people all over the world face have common elements and the interconnections must be recognized as they affect society as a whole. "The human community is one greater than any of its parts, greater than the separateness imposed by the various interest groups. It is the larger unity that is important and a comprehension of the things we have in common."[8] Economic education is just that. The problem it deals with cuts across compartments. Regardless of the initial problem, complete understanding will be achieved only when the student understands the entire process of analysis and evaluation. Economics cannot be studied in isolation, for political and social decisions determine the economic course to follow. Such relationships exist in other areas of study as well.

10. *Finally, the mood in the country today is to look upon education as a continuous, related process from Grades 1–12.* Growth in the student does not take place when education is conceived as materials added to the structure of the organism. Rather, growth is the incorporation of materials into the basic structure. Each person changes as he assimilates new material, and this change develops new needs and new capacities for growth. Assimilation depends on understanding, however. Each new experience is interpreted in terms of the old. Comprehension enables the growth to continue.

---

[7] Norman Cousins, *Who Speaks For Man?* (New York: The Macmillan Company, 1953), pp. 6–8.
[8] *Ibid.*, p. 8.

Research shows that growth follows a rather definite pattern which contains a sequential order of development as well as a rate of development. Any learning, if it is to be effective, must parallel the growth pattern of the individual and supply the necessary stimuli and materials needed by the maturational changes. The activities and the pace of instruction must be geared to the maturing capacities, abilities, and interests of the child. For example, economic problems are only the basic ideas of producing things, exchanging things, and consuming things. These can be taught in the second-grade project of a store or a unit on a farm or a dairy. The same thing can be taught at the senior level in high school, but this calls for greater experience and more understanding. "How can we allocate limited resources more equitably in meeting unlimited demands?" This is certainly more complicated than the earlier projects, but it does include what was learned in them.

Understanding in any area of knowledge can be thought of as an ascending and expanding spiral in which new learnings are incorporated into larger learnings.[9] At each stage in the educational process the learner is always confronted with experiences that challenge his increasing maturity, and he is forced to integrate his recent experiences, greatly enlarged and refined, into the original concepts that he learned in a simpler form in his earlier experiences.

These ten points are, then, the basic assumptions made in considering curriculum development in economic education. The discipline is enhanced when it views its contribution operating through these practices, but of greater importance is the recognition of the benefits to the learner of such considerations in the teaching process.

---

[9] *Teachers Guide To Developmental Economic Education Program, op. cit.*

CHAPTER V

Economics as a Discipline

Any body of knowledge has relevance only to the extent that it has meaning and usefulness to society. If knowledge can help the individual to live more fruitfully in the present, and plan more intelligently for the future, then serious consideration must be given to its inclusion as part of the formal education of every citizen in a democracy. The scientist and the mathematician have ably stated their case for the minimum understanding necessary for individuals living in the twentieth century, and because our existence depends to a large extent on these sciences, people have permitted many changes in the school curriculum to accommodate the emphasis on understanding the basic minimum of these disciplines. But in these areas a basic order of nature is being discovered bit by bit, and whether man approves of the knowledge or not, he must accept it and live by its implications. What man does with these discoveries is in another realm. But a vote of the majority cannot change the fact of fusion or fission.

When one deals with the social sciences an entirely different set of considerations enter the picture. The very term *behavioral sciences* explains the difference. Certainly, as disciplines open to study, they are of a later vintage than the sciences that deal with nature. But more important, they are sciences that have been developed by man to enable him to bring a sense of order out of the man-to-man existence in which he finds himself. Man is the subject of the social sciences, if "sciences" they may be called. Man has modified, discarded, created anew and discarded ideas, institutions, conceptions and traditions that have governed his behavior from the beginning. Because of this, the study of society and the individuals within it presents a different problem. But above all, the need for understanding man's actions is important beyond any other area of study and this is the case for the study of economics.

Of all of the social sciences, economics has perhaps made the greatest gains in developing a formalized structure which, if under-

stood, will help man to bring more order into his life. An analytical
structure has been developed that is based on a cause and effect relationship, yet takes into account the complexity and unpredictability
of man. Because of this, and because man's decisions in the area of
economics determine, to a great extent, the fullness of the life he will
lead, its relation to the school curriculum becomes highly important.

> The question is not whether to teach economics in the high
> schools; the only question (and it answers itself) is whether to do
> the job better than it is presently being done. It is as impossible to
> bypass economics in the high school as it is to avoid economic con-
> siderations in making political decisions at the level of citizenship.
> Any course in the social studies area, and many outside it, must
> necessarily bring economics into its range of discussion if it is to
> deal satisfactorily with its own principal subject matter. It is the eco-
> nomic understandings or misunderstandings gained in these courses
> as well as in "straight" courses in economics that emerge and take
> form in political decisions that may well be crucial for the per-
> formance and even the survival of our democratic institutions and
> ways.[1]

Economics for Citizenship

The subject matter of economics in the schools has been ably
presented in the framework developed by the National Task Force
in *Economic Education in the Schools.*[2] Four areas of analysis were
presented as being consistent with a minimal understanding necessary for "good citizenship and attainable by the high school graduate." Starting with the basic concept of scarcity, every economic
system is faced with the conflict that emerges due to the unlimited
wants of society and the limited resources which that society has
available. This is the basic economic problem. In every society the
factors of production, human and material, are scarce in relation to
the dreams and ambitions of people. Economic systems are thus developed to effectively and efficiently answer the question of, "How
do we bridge the gap?"

Economics, therefore, concerns itself with the study of allocating
scarce resources in such a way that optimum satisfaction results. In
our economic system the answers to, "Who shall produce how much

---

[1] "Economics in the Schools," *American Economic Review,* Vol. 53, No. 1,
Part 2, Supplement (March, 1963).

[2] *Economic Education in the Schools, op. cit.*

of what?" "How shall our resources be combined to produce those goods and services we want?" and "Who shall get how much of the resulting product?" are determined by the market. Therefore, the study of how individual decisions and competition determine price, production, and consumption is one of the most important segments of economics.

Further, the study of economics should enable the students to analyze causal relationships and utilize them to investigate problem areas of primary concern to society. The Task Force therefore stressed, in addition to the analysis of the basic understanding of scarcity and allocation of resources, the need for comprehension on the part of students of how to obtain growth and stability, and how the resultant product of the people shall be distributed. The latter question is one that perhaps causes the greatest disagreement among the people. Finally, an understanding of how other economic systems operate to solve their major economic problems was considered by the Task Force to be a necessity for citizen understanding.

It is difficult in reading the introductory books on economics to clearly grasp what is the "analysis" that the economist talks about constantly. Certainly, the analysis is evident to the professional, but not so for the uninitiated. This represents, perhaps, the most difficult handicap for those who desire to improve their ability to utilize economic analysis in their every day life. This would suggest an approach similar to that utilized in the TV course "The American Economy"[3] or in the television series by the Columbia Broadcasting System entitled "Money Talks."[4]

Another approach to developing this understanding is through the economic objectives and problems which are contained in the American system. First, every system is concerned with efficiency in producing the things it needs. Each system tries to maximize the satisfaction of wants with the least possible expenditure of resources —land, labor, capital, men, and machines. The economist refers to achieving the best output-input relationship. Production, distribution of product exchange, organization and administration of business, and individual motivation are part of this objective.

---

[3] "The American Economy," *op. cit.*

[4] "Money Talks," transcript and description of five broadcasts produced by CBS Television August 20–24, 1962. (Available from The Calvin K. Kazanjian Economics Foundation, Wilton, Connecticut).

Second, a fair distribution of the results of the efficient production among all engaged in this production is necessary. This involves a determination of wages, salaries, and fees, an adequate compensation in the form of rent or profits for those who own the land and capital goods, and an adequate return in the form of interest and profit for those who have used their savings for investment purposes.

Third, there is a necessity for continued technological advance to insure increasing efficiency. Growth, as an element of this continued process to maintain a healthy economy, requires incentives, experimentation, initiative, and education.

Another objective is maintaining relative stability over a period of time. Avoidance of fluctuations in the economy and the provision of opportunity for each individual to achieve a maximum of income security consistent with his talents have been of increasing concern since the depression of the 1930's.

Finally, all of the above objectives are viewed within the framework of their conformity to general social values, namely, equality of opportunity, democracy in social organization and operation, and individual freedom.

These objectives are not independent of one another but directly interrelated. This very fact gives rise to the emphasis on economics for citizenship. These interrelationships of the different values citizens have determine the objectives which the economic system will accomplish. In a democratic society, such goals or objectives are in competition with one another and the interrelationship between them, or the emphasis on any one, depends upon the knowledge of the subject matter and upon the analytic faculties of the citizens. The final objective of any economic system is to achieve the happiest and most productive blending or balance of all the objectives above. This effort gives rise to the important problems which come out of these attempts to reach the objectives.

In attempting to achieve the most efficient production, the utilization of resources for the long or short run becomes a paramount issue. Imperfections in the competitive mechanism in the form of monopolies, the lack of mobility of the factors of production, degree of education, governmental and private hinderances to trade, and the extensions of governmental regulation must be considered in arriving at any policy decision. Also, there is a possible conflict between individual security and competitive efficiency, the degree of planning necessary to achieve the end, and the flexibility and stability of the money system.

In achieving a fair distribution of output, the definitions of the word "fair" are many. Incentives may be at variance with the efficiency concept. Decisions arrived at through collective bargaining, lobbying, government subsidies and price supports, legislation restricting competition, and the increase or decrease of educational opportunities are important. An additional consideration is the question of a suitable tax policy.

Technological advance brings with it many problems also; for instance, how fast can the economy grow without bringing about instability is a constant point of conflict. Innovations may cause unwanted disturbances in the economy. Individual security is also challenged by technological change, and the balance between materialistic and aesthetic values becomes precarious. The psychological and sociological factors are important elements to decision-making.

The problems involved in achieving economic stability for the long run are many and difficult. The causes of business fluctuations are many, and sometimes uncertain. Measures proposed to achieve stability may limit economic freedom. The imposition of monetary or direct controls, the relative amounts of social or private insurance for individual security, and the interrelation between such security and efficiency are factors that weigh heavily in making economic decisions.

And finally, the conformity of the economic system to general social values, the conflicting definitions of these values, their paradoxical nature, and the relation between public policy and individual freedom are continually being re-evaluated.

Once again, this demonstrates why economics is an ideal subject for the classroom, both from the methodological and content aspects. Relationships, cause and effect, a process of reasoning, a need for balance and, eventually, a wise choosing of alternatives is implicit in the discipline itself. Each of the objectives above gives rise to many problems and these problems provide the motivation and procedural approach for both student and teacher.

Methodology of Economics

"The most important step toward understanding in economics—as in other branches of knowledge—is the replacement of emotional, unreasoned judgments by objective, rational analysis. This is the first lesson to be learned in approaching the study of economics."[5] Reasoning of this type does not come about automatically. Rather, students must be given an opportunity to develop the method of thinking that is used in science and economic research.

It is assumed that young people as well as adults are concerned about, and interested in, the major problems confronting society since these problems have a direct relationship to peoples' immediate needs. Perhaps the relationship between the personal and the institutional aspects of the problem is not readily apparent, but it is possible to relate these, by careful analysis, to the broader and deeper implications which flow from them.[6]

The "problem approach" in education, then, has a major role in the development of a dynamic society. Such a technique can only operate in a society where people have the responsibility for decision-making and where such decisions are based on what is best for the general welfare. The process involved is in keeping with the times. Decision-making suitable to the environment in which it is circumscribed provides the strength for a continuation of a society. If Noah Webster's statement, "If we are to educate for a democracy, it must be by an education suited to a democracy" is accepted, then the problems approach must be given high priority in education.[7]

The relation of public policy to an economic and political system creates the problems which it is possible to solve intelligently only by a technique designed to develop objective understanding. Traditional methods in education apparently have not succeeded in coping with this problem. Here the opportunity exists for developing the potentialities of the individual to the utmost by providing means to conduct a study of the students' own choosing. Modern economics is a complexiy of problems, and therefore suited ideally for such a method. Taking the concern of the student as a motivation for a

---

[5] *Economic Education in the Schools, op. cit.,* p. 14.

[6] *Developing Personal Economic Competence Through Economic Education* (New York: Joint Council on Economic Education, 1964).

[7] Arthur D. Hollingshead, *Guidance in Democratic Living* (New York: Appleton-Century-Crofts, 1941) p. 1.

study of economics and relating this to the content area which is ideally adapted to a "problems approach" makes it possible for a teacher to consider each student as an individual and assist him in gaining understanding for his own concern.

Nourse presents the value of the "problem approach" excellently.

"Problem" has become, for the educationists, a word of art. In their usage it has come to signify the doorway through which we, all of us—but adolescents, in particular—may pass from the shadowy chamber of the mysterious and the frustrating into the bright outer world of understanding adjustment and social contribution. The child turns to his elders with the question, "What is that?" or "How come?" or "Why did this happen?" or "When will that happen again?" As a novice at life he sees it only as a jumble of episodes or discreet phenomena. But understanding of life or any of its major aspects is achieved only when we see it as a process whose parts have meaningful relations one to another. At first the child takes all the answers he gets from adults as authentic explosions of knowledge. Later, he perceives that some of these answers are utter duds, whereas others are 'trigger mechanisms' that start chain reactions, releasing the atomic power of original and even creative thought. From the idle question the learner proceeds to the propounding of significant problems—about his world and his position in it.[8]

Senesh comments in even greater detail on this thesis by stating that the basic purpose in problem-solving is:

. . . to help the students recognize, through their experiences, the existence of a problem, to enable them to analyze the problem, find alternative solutions, and choose from among these solutions intelligently. These are precisely the capabilities required of citizens if we are to maintain a democracy of high order and progress toward those social objectives of economic growth, stability, and security.

The problem-solving approach is a method which has no significance unless it achieves fundamental understanding, factual knowledge, and disciplined thinking in the subject field. Methodology and knowledge of the subject matter are inseparable. Economic education must not fail to equip students with the tools of economic analysis and with the knowledge of the problem area which will enable them to distinguish between personal and social problems and to evaluate alternative policies in terms of their impact upon the economy as a whole and its various segments. It must also help pupils to recognize the part played by individual and concerted action in the solution of these problems.

---

[8] Nourse, *Persistent Problems of The American Economy, op. cit.,* p. 297.

Such training must be provided to students at the public school level, since only a minority attend college. And it must be provided by giving students experience in dealing with actual and significant problems that confront society. Topics cannot be sacrificed because they are difficult; rather it is the responsibility of the teacher to find a method of presentation which will put them in the students' terms. It is methodology, more than subject matter, which must be chosen in terms of the interest and maturity of the pupils.[9]

By such an approach, the potentialities of youth are improved to enable him to function more effectively in his daily economic activity. He becomes a participant in a long-range program for his own self-interest and general welfare. He alone makes the decision on what economic structure best serves the general welfare. As a participant in decision-making he will share and shape progress and be a part of all he surveys.

Economics taught by such a method is thought of as an order created by humans with a set of social and national interests. If education can insure that all citizens as individuals will seek that which is best for the national interest, then society would be secure from pressure politics. But where selfish group interest is predominant, society can expect pressure. What may result from special interest group pressures is a pork-barrel policy and this is not necessarily in the national interest and may be inconsistent with it. When any special interest group predominates, society may be deprived of that which is best for the national welfare.

Such a policy has led to propaganda, half-truths, political issues established by emotion, and rule by vested interests anxious to keep the public ignorant and susceptible to pat conclusions. Democracy needs an enlightened public as well as the expert. Citizens must be able to distinguish between policies so that support may be given to the one which is in the national interest, for that is the policy more nearly right.

An understanding of the basic economic problem is, as previously stated, a partial answer to the question of minimum understanding. But, if there is to be the most satisfactory allocation, this would require a knowledge of the distinctive qualities and features of the economic system doing the allocating. Intelligent action fur-

---

9 Lawrence Senesh, *International Trade* (New York: Joint Council on Economic Education, 1953), pp. 32–33.

ther requires that every one be acquainted with the institutions and attitudes which make the economy work. In our society, institutions that do exist, do so because people need and want them. Each institution has been established to make society behave in a certain way. In the realm of economics the following institutions pattern and shape our "economic" society:

1. Private property
2. Freedom of contract; the right to assume obligations
3. Productive resources organized and used by private business firms or organizations
4. Individual self-interest as a motive for economic behavior
5. The market place and a medium of exchange coupled with the other institutions which provide the chief means of making economic decisions in America
6. The government as the balance wheel of the economy, policing and directing each of the above institutions.

Problems cannot be avoided, however. Many problems originate in the nature of the institutions mentioned above. Minimum essentials of economic understanding would require that people need to know how to analyze such problems and see them in relationship to the basic one. The economist calls this economic analysis, but the educator interprets it as the "problems approach." The alternative to seeking solutions by the problems approach is to act arbitrarily or reach them authoritatively.

A clear definition of each problem, understandable by all, must be formulated, the pitfalls of faulty logic avoided, and research conducted and motivated by objectivity. False conclusions should not be drawn from statistics. Hypotheses should be established and assumptions explicitly stated. Alternative solutions should be considered, and every decision made in the light of the prevailing factors subject to change as the factors change.

Lewis E. Wagner summarizes from his research the conclusions on what a well-informed citizen needs to know about the American economy. First, each should know what an economic system is and be aware of the functions it performs. Such knowledge would make evident the reason for the existence of an economic system in any type of political society. Secondly, each citizen should be informed about the structure of the institutions that exist in the American society to organize and guide the economic activity. Thirdly, each person should have sufficient knowledge to evaluate how well the economic system is performing. This would require a familiarity with, and an understanding of, "the yardsticks which have been developed" for measuring the performance of the economy. And last, each should be cognizant of the factors which determine the course of economic activity. Knowledge of "how the various cogs of the economic machine mesh" contributes to such understanding and allows insight into "what determines the rate of activity."[10]

The Relationship of Theory to Economic Education

Too often educators are prone to reject the importance of theory in the educational process. Failure seems to be related in the minds of many with the offhand comment that "it is too theoretical." Pragmatism has been misinterpreted so that what is practical is not deemed to have any relationship to theory.

An analysis of this kind of thinking makes its fallaciousness very evident. All people operate on theory whenever thought is applied prior to action. Generalizations which we live by are the result of repeated experiences, and these constitute the tests which are necessary in the formulation of any theory.

Practice can only be evaluated if it can be evaluated in light of theory. Nourse points out that "there is nothing so practical as a good theory—that is, a generalization based on a wide and precise observation rather than on limited personal experience and snap judgments of the 'practical' man."[11]

Dewey also expressed his belief in the necessity of being informed about theory.

> Theory is in the end . . . the most practical of all things, because the widening of the range of attention beyond nearby purpose and desire eventually results in the creation of wider and farther reaching purposes and enables us to make use of a much wider and deeper range of conditions and means than were expressed in the observation of primitive practical purposes.

[10] Lewis E. Wagner, *Measuring the Performance of the Economy, A Primer of Economics, No. 3* (Iowa City: Bureau of Business and Economic Research, State University of Iowa, 1963), p. 2.

[11] Edwin G. Nourse, *Economics in the Public Service,* (New York: Harcourt, Brace & World, Inc., 1953), p. 9.

> Facts which are . . . interrelated form a system, a science. The practitioner who knows the system . . . is evidently in possession of a powerful instrument for observing and interpreting what goes on before him. The intellectual tool affects his attitudes and modes of response in what he does. Because the range of understanding is deepened and widened, he can take into account remote consequences which were originally hidden from view, and, hence were ignored in his actions. Greater continuity is introduced; he does not isolate situations and deal with them in separation as he was compelled to do when ignorant of connecting principles. At the same time, his practical dealings became more flexible. Seeing more relations he sees more possibilities, more opportunities. He is emancipated from the need of following tradition and special precedents. His ability to judge being enriched, he has a wider range of alternatives to select from in dealing with individual situations.[12]

There is little question about the fact that education should concern itself with practical problems. But educators cannot identify or define the actual problem without proper orientation to theory. Neither can they teach for the moment, but rather they must lead youth to see the immediate in relation to the theories that have been developed out of the many "immediates" of the past. Growth, stability, security and economic freedom are goals, the attainment of which introduces many problems. But when discussion centers around capitalism vs. socialism, the "welfare state," inflation, taxation, prices, unemployment, agriculture, etc., we are considering aspects of the basic problem which can only be understood as the basic program is understood. How to maintain growth or any other of the goals mentioned is a theoretical concept, and it is on these theories that our policy-makers determine public and private action.

Whitehead is even more emphatic in his insistence on education being concerned with theoretical concepts.

> . . . theoretical ideas should always find important applications within the pupil's curriculum. This is not an easy doctrine to apply, but a very hard one. It contains within itself the problem of keeping knowledge alive, of preventing it from becoming inert, which is the central problem of all education.[13]

Economic problems cannot be solved by emotional or biased

---

12 John Dewey, *The Sources of a Science of Education* (New York: Liveright Publishing Corp. 1929), pp. 17–21.

13 Alfred Whitehead, *Aims of Education* (New York: The Macmillan Company, 1959), p. 7.

thinking. There is an orderly and objective procedure which must be followed. It is in the adherence to this procedure that the economist qualifies as a scientist. The search for facts is paramount, and once having secured these facts, an economist searches for a common pattern which exists among them. These patterns of uniformity may be termed "models." Actually, they are generalizations which have been formulated to express the patterns which have evolved from previous experience. In essence, they are theories.

Most of the difficulties which critics have with the involvement of theory in the learning process stem from the fact that people do not understand why theories are necessary. They do not understand the limitations theories possess, the uses to which they may be put, or even the true nature of a theory. All students claim to be searching for the facts without recognizing that facts do not stand in isolation from each other, but exist in a relationship that produces meaning. Alone, facts have little utility, for their use depends on their being integrated into a coordinated frame of reference. Theory creates the order out of the great wealth of facts which the world possesses and allows for interpretations to be made which are relative to the problems that instigated the search for the facts.

Knowledge is gained through such a process. Practical activity is evaluated in light of this knowledge which in turn passes on into theoretical activity and manifests itself once again in practical activity. By way of illustration, there is a theory in economics which states that as income increases, consumer spending increases also, but at a rate of increase which is less than the income increase. The facts of research and national experience tend to support this theory, but such a theory does cast a different light on the interpretation of savings in relation to increased wages.

Knowledge then is the end product of theorizing and "involves the establishment of relations of dependence between what is thus directly experienced and what is not."[14] What these relations are, however, is not to be settled by intuition or authority, whether the problem under consideration involves issues of physics, private morality, or public policy. It is above all, a matter requiring reflective thought or experimental inquiry.

Theories are general modes of activity that provide a pattern of

---

[14] Ernest Nagel, "Pure Science and Gross Experience," *New Republic* (October 17, 1949), p. 22.

relationships drawn from experience. Theories supply the framework for evaluating and projecting change.

Obviously then, economic activity cannot be expected to coincide with theory on every issue, but this in no way changes the theory. Economic policy is determined on aggregate behavior and it is necessary for each person to observe his personal behavior in light of its effect on the aggregate. When the positions are reversed, this gives rise to the emotional biases and prejudices so prevalent in the field of economics.

The Role of Values in Economic Education

A discussion of economic education would not be complete without some consideration of the role of values in such a study. No other single factor seems to cause greater disagreement among those in the profession. It is precisely at this point that the economist appears to part company with the educator, but, in reality, the difficulty seems to be semantic more than anything else. Confusion takes place in attempting to determine where analysis ends and value judgments begin, or, if other terms are preferred, how means are distinguished from the ends.

Perhaps Einstein can clarify this issue from the point of view of a scientist.

> Whatever this tool [scientific method] in the hand of man will produce depends entirely on the nature of the goals alive in this mankind. Once the goals exist, the scientific method furnishes the means to realize them. Yet it cannot furnish the very goals. The scientific method itself would not even have led anywhere, it would not have been born without a passionate striving for clear understanding. Perfections of means and confusion of goals seem . . . to characterize our age.[15]

There are many economists who would endorse this point of view without qualification. To them economics is a science and not an ethical system. This is not to infer that values are not important to them or that these do not constitute a major aspect of educational responsibility. But the interpretation suggested would be that the study of economics would enable everyone to select the course of

---

[15] Albert Einstein, *Out of My Later Years* (New York: Philosophical Library, 1950), p. 113.

action from among the alternatives that would be in line with the values he holds. A better hope is projected here, for this process permits a change in a person's value as well. Without such freedom a type of authoritarianism would be possible. Confusion might result in determining whether the basic value was to be freedom in a society which allows for economic freedom or an economic system which determines the freedom which society is to have.

Developing the ability in students to reason analytically may well bring about a change in their basic beliefs. Free inquiry as opposed to any blind acceptance of dogma must be maintained. Each person should be respected sufficiently as an individual to develop his own sense of values based upon his inquiry and experience.

As a scientist the economist "excludes from his consideration all factors that are noneconomic—aesthetic, ethical, . . . 'subjective,' or broadly . . . 'political.' The economic engineer . . . decide[s] what, in the light of current knowledge, is the course of action which will direct practices or modify structures in such a way as to promote economic stability and progress [society's values], taking into account such other factors of the human process as he or his employer thinks is desirable to have recognized."[16]

The individual citizen, whatever his status, is in a position to take the technical advice and make the policy judgments that may mean a choice between conflicting values but reflect what is most suitable in the total situation. The citizen must, through policy, "adjust [its] pace to the rate at which a society or the group can assimilate social change. To be really workable or practical in the long run [policy] must not make compromises with economic principles to serve some special purpose or selfish end."[17]

An argument could be made that democracy as a system, with its emphasis on freedom and a responsibility of its citizens to make and revise its laws, made the entire question of value judgments important. Where the state gave up its decision-making powers to social institutions, the decisions were the result of the values held by these people. If a society is to be organized and directed by such institutions, value judgments become crucial in terms of the goals which have been set by free decisions. Progress can be measured only against these goals and is defined accordingly.

[16] Edwin G. Nourse, *Economics in the Public Service, op. cit.,* p. 17.
[17] *Ibid,* p. 18.

In an open society the crucial matter is whether young people are to be taught that truth and right are progressively discovered by free inquiry or are to be indoctrinated with some dogma. Obviously, there can be but one answer to this in a democratic society and the first alternative above meets the qualifications.

C. E. Ayres supports this thesis in his interpretation of John Dewey's instrumentalism. Of course, Dewey challenges absolutism in any sense. If "values" are to be conceived as "ends" then one accepts the "means to ends" relationship. Tradition has forced most people into this type of thinking. Examination of this fact, however, indicates that our behavior is not related to some remote end. Rather, according to Ayres, "day-to-day experience reveals no generic difference between 'ends' and 'means.' Every . . . item of our experience is both an end and a means [and] 'means' and 'ends' can [not] be distingushed . . ." in our every day actions. "Values have the significance of process, not of substance or essence." It is this "continuous, developmental process from which all the achievements of mankind have flowed" that runs all through human behavior. "This . . . is what Dewey has called the instrumental process" and is termed by him as "identical with technology for the economist. Hence the continued and maximal growth of technology provides an objective, factual criterion of economic value that is not a matter of taste at all," and leads to the conclusion that "existing resources should be so allocated that there will be continually more to allocate."[18]

Dewey has resolved the semantic difficulty in making value a matter of process and not essence. This eliminates thinking in terms of "ends" and, according to Ayres, relates our thinking to how we actually do think.

From the above discussion, it can be seen that the point of view set forth here is that if values are accepted as authoritarian and imposed, they cannot be part of the economist's professional role. If, however, values as such are a part of a process, formulated and reformulated on the basis of everyday experience and predicated on goals which are agreed to continuously by the body politic, then they are part of the economist's thinking.

---

[18] C. E. Ayres, "Instrumental Economics," *New Republic* (October 17, 1949), p. 19.

> The most representative economic theorist of any particular period is one who . . . presents a discerning description and plausible rationale for an existing economic system. His analysis represents the point of view of the majority or what one may call the "overworld" of economic theorists . . . But as the economic, political, and social atmosphere . . . and as the institutional framework begins to change, economic theory also undergoes a gradual transformation. Skepticism regarding many of the economic laws espoused by the majority gains ground and sometimes the "heresies" of the minority attain such general acceptance that the majority opinion passes into the limbo of historical residue, leaving for posterity only a small part of what had allegedly been a comprehensive economic analysis.[19]

A typical example of content analysis, methodology, values, and theory relationships that could well be followed by teachers in many areas of economics can be built around the farm problem in the United States. Even a brief analysis of such a broad issue would be a big undertaking. It would involve at least three treatments: one dealing with the causes of low farm incomes, the second dealing with the reactions of farmers to those low incomes, and the third dealing with the implications of the significance of those reactions not only to the farm sector but also to the economy as a whole. Such an analysis was well presented in the report "Economics in the Schools."[20]

The second section of that analysis, following an explanation of why farm incomes are low, will illustrate what good analysis involves. It is as follows:

> THE REACTIONS OF FARMERS TO LOW INCOMES. Observers of the agricultural sector of the economy can easily detect at least six reasonably important reactions by the farm community to declining farm incomes.
>
> First, individual farmers will each see the necessity of investing additional funds in new cost-reducing machinery and equipment and—as each sees a portion of his time unemployed or ill-used on farms which are too small as output per hour rises using the new machinery and methods—in additional land. Since each farmer is likely to have limited financial resources, each will clamor for additional credit to be made available on favorable terms. Thus, be-

---

[19] E. A. Johnson and Herman E. Kroos, *The American Economy, Its Origins, Development and Transformation* (Englewood Cliffs, N.J.: Prentice-Hall, Inc., 1960), pp. 415–416.

[20] "Economics in the Schools," *American Economic Review, op. cit.,* pp. 13–18.

ginning as early as the twenties, a succession of special programs and agencies for "easy credit" to farmers has appeared.

Second, farmers will see prices paid for needed farm inputs as "too high." This view will be particularly strong the larger the size of firms with which the farmer deals. The cry of "monopoly" will then be raised. . . . As a result, farmers have generally supported railroad rate and service regulation and vigorous antimonopoly laws and their administration, and participated actively in the development and use of co-operatives in an attempt to obtain needed farm and consumer inputs at lower prices.

Third, farmers will from time to time, attribute their low incomes to inadequate efforts and programs to expand markets, and will look toward market-expanding activities on both domestic and foreign fronts. Domestically, farmers have sought expansion of demand by encouraging research directed toward the industrial use of farm products and attempts to develop improved products (e.g., leaner pork) and thus expand consumption. With regard to exports, farmers have looked to improved marketing techniques and products to stimulate overseas sales, lower United States tariffs on nonagricultural products to enable other nations to sell more to the United States and, thus, earn dollars to buy United States farm products, and relief and/or development shipments of farm products abroad on either a gift or loan basis.

Fourth, farmers will see prices obtained for their products as "too low." They will ask for higher prices guaranteed by a sympathetic government. But, to obtain these higher prices, the quantity of farm products actually going to the market to be sold must be reduced. This can be done either by storage of some part of the marketable output (hoping for better market conditions—and higher prices for expanded marketings—at some future date), or by restrictions on production. Thus, agriculture has witnessed a variety of "price support" programs coupled with attempts at reduction of supplies via storage programs, acreage restrictions, the "soil bank," and the like.

Fifth, farmers will see prices of food and fiber as falling rapidly as markets thin during depressions. Farmers thus have a special reason to regard business slumps as undesirable, and it is not surprising to find farm organizations as active supporters of stabilizing monetary and fiscal policies. More than this, price support and storage programs have sometimes been seen as proper only for periods of unusually low farm prices and incomes during recessions—with stored accumulations to be sold at higher prices during subsequent booms.

Sixth, farmers leave agriculture for higher income, nonfarm jobs. Since this is most easily done when nonfarm employment is high during prosperity, this reaction to low incomes depends also upon the maintenance of high levels of economic activity. It also requires adequate funds to finance the move, and the acquisition of necessary education, training, and skills to allow the ex-farm person to compete successfully in urban areas.

To complete the analysis of the whole problem the above sections would need to be followed by discussions and investigations into the consequences of farm reactions and the relationship of the farm problem to the economy as a whole.

The illustration has several pertinent comments to make on teaching economics which should be of value for anyone with responsibilities for the teaching of economics:

1. Decision-makers (in this case, farmers) respond to opportunities defined for them by prices (of goods sold, of inputs purchased) determined in the market place. Students can see that what and how much farmers produce and the techniques of production selected depend upon these market-determined price alternatives. They can observe directly how a system of prices and markets organizes economic activity.

2. Optimum response by individual farmers to price alternatives leads to over-all low incomes in agriculture and therefore both to group (largely governmental) actions to modify market alternatives and to movement of resources into other more promising sectors of the economy. Students can see a government response to dissatisfaction by a politically powerful economic group. They can also witness the discipline of a market-organized society as it both pushes persons from agriculture and pulls them into alternative economic activities.

3. The consequences of government actions must be interpreted within the framework embracing their impact on market alternatives. Thus a government action making credit favorably available to farmers to add to their capital facilities leads to market alternatives further reducing returns to farm labor. Or, price support programs both increase difficulties in competing in export markets and create programs of mounting surpluses of agricultural products. (Incidentally, the surpluses are a consequence of an attempt to solve the fundamental farm problem—that of low farm incomes. They are not the farm problem.)

4. The well-being of any sector of the economy is strongly influenced by the over-all health of the economy. Thus the student can see the farmer as better off if he moves from the farm if the economy is characterized by prosperity, not recession.

5. The decline of one sector of the economy (in this case agriculture) is not inconsistent with growth in the entire economy.

It should be possible to apply elementary economic theory in a similar way to other problems. Such a development of theory would provide the basis for much more adequate analysis than that now available. The essentials of macro-economics might well be developed in terms of the circular flow of income and expenditures. Perhaps the concept of equilibrium should be avoided, but enough can be done in this area to build a background for the study of economic stability and growth. Facts on the distribution and stability of national income could be presented as groundwork for theoretical analysis. The relation between the supply of money and the price level also would seem to be a possible subject for analysis at the elementary level. Descriptive analysis (such as that attempted above with the farm problem), if pointed directly to the solution of some vital problem, could be made more meaningful. . . . Description should be approached from an analytical point of view so that a limited cause and effect theorizing may be undertaken. From analysis of this sort the student should learn that when he thinks about economics, he must continually ask himself, "Why?" If he persistently raises this question with himself, he will be well along the way toward understanding the need for cause and effect analysis in economics.[21]

---

[21] *Ibid.*

CHAPTER VI

Economics in the School Curriculum

Any curriculum developed by a school system must necessarily be based on certain assumptions considered to be effective in the learning process. In recent years much thought has been given to the relation of content to the experiences and maturity of the child. Research and experiences have clearly indicated that the ability of young people to deal with abstractions and analysis goes far beyond the expectancies which have existed for many years. There is little in economics which cannot be grasped by children at any age as long as the concepts are related to the maturity of the youngster. Bruner in his work in science education, Beberman in mathematics, and Senesh in economics have provided evidence to substantiate the efficacy of conceptual learning.

The experiences of children provide the starting point for economic education (and the essential analytical framework of the economic system can be found in these experiences). The framework remains the same whether we are concerned with the world as seen through the eyes of the six-year-old or the adult. There is a spiral effect. In each succeeding year in school the basic concepts are expanded and deepened to challenge the increasing maturity of the child.

Senesh, for example, raised the question of relating the child's experiences in the first grade to this larger framework of the conflict of unlimited wants and scarce resources; the method of meeting the challenge of this conflict; the ways that societies take to determine what is to be produced, how much, and how and who will receive the product. The concept of free choice in determining the answers to these questions is part of the market and price system which in turn is related to the values which people have.

> Children and teacher [in the first grade] for example, may discuss what they would like to have for Christmas and how these choices have to be limited because of the size of the family income and because of the desires of other members of the family. Through a

series of exercises in choice-making, children can discover that individuals, neighborhoods, cities and nations all have to make choices for the same reasons. Watching machines work, or observing the efforts to initiate space travel, are good experiences to dramatize the role of invention and technology in closing the gap between unlimited wants and limited resources. The fact that homes run better when certain members of the family are responsible for certain duties and that school affairs operate more smoothly when certain persons are responsible for certain duties, . . . are examples of the division of labor and specialization. This shows how the division of labor and the organization process increases productivity. First graders may discuss how they will use their allowances and how prices and the size of their allowances affect their decisions of what to buy and how much. They can grasp that their decisions to buy hula hoops instead of candy bars, along with the decisions of other people, will decide how many hula hoops will be produced, how many candy bars, and in the same way, how many automobiles, and how many houses.[1]

By the same procedures, the necessity of government programs and taxes can be related to family members who are not producers and to the services which all enjoy in return for tax payments.

The philosophy upon which a scope and sequence arrangement for the schools may be built is one in which the concepts introduced at the first grade are not terminal but rather open many doors for increased understanding. A number of school systems have developed such programs and a great deal of similarity appears in their reports. The elementary school program, therefore, would seem to follow the pattern below.

Grade 1—Home and family activities. Family life as the first-grader knows it and family life in other cultures enables the child to realize the roles and responsibilities this social unit illustrates. Division of labor, specialization, and interdependence are clearly presented. The efficiency created by technological developments, the differences between consumers and producers, the understanding of income and the factors of production are further explored, and the relationship between productivity and income established.

Grade 2—The child's immediate community or neighborhood. Moving into a more complex social unit, the environment of the

---

[1] Lawrence Senesh, "The Organic Curriculum: A New Experiment in Economic Education," *The Councilor* (Illinois Council for the Social Studies, March, 1960), pp. 45–46.

community, permits the second-grader to further develop the concepts acquired in Grade 1. Contrasts and comparisons are possible. The decision-making role of the individual becomes more impersonal and the individual's contributions are viewed from another angle—the benefit not only to himself and the family but also to his neighbors and their neighbors. In economics, the specializations of communities are emphasized, interdependence becomes more important, work specialization leads to a consideration of money as a medium of exchange, the supply and demand side of the market can be seen through the eyes of the consumer, and profits can be related to capital investment seen through the occupations of parents. Through the study of occupations, the second-graders can develop insights into community location and the type of jobs available, the relative compensation for a variety of jobs, the relationship of productivity and income to education and technology, and its resultant effect on the community as a whole.

Grade 3—The larger encompassing community and its counterparts in the nation. Again, contrasts and comparisons are possible. Third-graders see the workers of any community as parts of an industrial establishment which produces products more advantageously than some other community. Exchanging these specialties introduces the economics of transportation and trade. The circular flow of money can be introduced to show the relation between income, employment, and production, thus enabling specialization to operate. Specialization can be related to the efficient allocation of resources to gain the best return. Children come to realize that the producers in the community are always faced with the choice of how to use their scarce resources. Community development can be understood and growth of one community can be contrasted with decline in another.

Grades 4–6—The state and the nation in its regional and world setting. The pattern at this level remains rather definitive but the grade placement loses its sharpness. Basic concepts in those three years, however, should emphasize how within each political unit man utilizes the resources at his disposal to bring about the greatest satisfaction of wants. Differences exist in various areas because people are motivated by different desires and values. In seeking to satisfy these, specialization develops based upon the natural resources, the geographical factors, the human resources, the transportation and communication available, and the cultural determinants. These factors determine demand and production operating within the economic system of the country.

Regional study should focus on the economic specialties of the area, the reasons why these developed, and the reasons for economic change can be assessed. As resources have become more available, markets and products have changed. Transportation is seen as a vital factor in change and the increase or decrease of supply and demand can be related to this. Projections can be made as to the future economic activity of the community or area. Communities within an area or outside of the area can be assessed for their similarities and their differences.

Changes in occupational or economic structure can be seen in light of the profit potential and the changing market. Trade can be explored as the possible lifeline to growth, stability, and security in a community. Students can thus gain understanding of the relationship of their immediate world to the world as a whole.

To illustrate—Why has the South changed from a cotton to a cattle economy, then to textile production, chemical manufacture, and diversified manufacturing? Finding answers to this question can lead to a comprehensive study of economics. Studies which investigate why areas have specialized in certain products or services, why certain industries have located in specific spots, and why urban centers have developed where they have introduce the student to what the economist terms *location theory* but within the basic framework of the market and price system.

Grade 7—World geography. Such courses are usually organized on a regional basis. The experiences the student undergoes can certainly be called "hopscotching around the world." One approach is to start with a study of the United Nations and its membership, the various blocs that make up the constituency, and the problems that have to be faced due to the geographic differentiation. The UNESCO studies provide almost an outline for such a course. An approach, continent by continent, may also be used, and still a third, that of following the trade relationships of the United States is an interesting approach.

The nature and size of business operations can be related to some extent to the geographical conditions existing in each area. Locational differentiation can be plotted out. Comparisons can be made of employment, population, and income. The activities of each government can be studied and analyzed based on these comparisons.

There are also excellent possibilities in looking at the economic security picture for families in the U.S. and contrasting this security with the situation of corresponding units in other countries. The various roles of the individual, the private organizations with which the individual has a relationship, and the government should be examined.

Economic development and cooperation of the nations of the world is the goal of the United Nations. Efforts to achieve these are detailed in many publications. The elements of communism and socialism can be examined as a means of achieving growth in comparison with capitalism in the United States. Resource-use studies can be made and findings related to economic development. Comparative advantage as a theory becomes evident, and specialization and interdependence on a world scale can be demonstrated. Some nations provide fine examples of human resources overcoming a deficiency of natural resources. Population growth rate can be seen in bold relief against the standard of living of nations. To this list may be added many other concepts but perhaps as important as any is the realization by young people that a variety of factors such as human and natural resources, cultural tradition, political organization, the psychological outlook, education, communication and transportation, available capital, and religious values determine the economic status of any land.

Every nation in the world is concerned with economic problems. There is a geographical relationship to such problems but the answer will not be found in these factors alone. But, if geography is to be more than a study of unrelated facts and maps, and if it is to be related to people and their concerns, then it must concern itself with economics, for this area of study gives meaning and purpose for understanding people and conditions of living in other lands.

Grade 8—United States history. Traditionally, this is the subject that has been offered at the eighth-grade level. More recently there has been a strong tendency to present to the student the emergence of America as the united nation that brought the people, in 1865, to the threshold of political, economic, and social gains that are still evolving. Emphasis is also given to studying the history of the state. Both areas of study permit much emphasis on economics and provide an immediacy that had been lacking for those young people.

United States history is related to geography as well. The development of new areas and new resources and the interregional struggles brought many shifts in the social patterns of the people. Variations in economic activities, greater economic opportunities, and specialized occupations can be closely related to the market place. A study of economic activities in the colonial period, for example, illustrates the concept of scarcity and provides the vehicle for considering the economic goals of our society.

Students can concentrate "on gathering information about the ways in which the colonists made a living, the types of homes in which they lived, the kinds of food they were able to produce and buy, the different kinds of clothing produced, the varieties of trade practiced and industries established, and the different institutions developed to increase trade."[2] The concept of economic growth is the subject of study. Trade relations lead to a study of competition, the role of taxation, and the determinants of trades. The elements of balance of payments are possible understandings to develop.

Through the study of noted individuals in American history, contributions to the improvement of production, distribution, consumption and exchange can be noted. The development of new industries can be examined in light of the market.

The Puritans' frugality can be related to capital formation; the Hamiltonian-Jeffersonian controversies are studies in economic growth and freedom; and the concern of the Jacksonians over centralized banking are all possibilities for introducing economic concepts into the early history of America.

Similarly, when studying state history the same concepts can be introduced. Exploration within a state can be related to motivation for economic activity. Settlement is related to natural resources and specialization and exchange can be seen in its early formation. The role of the government in economic life had its beginnings in the early days and all of these concepts can be traced through the developments within each state.

The only limitation that exists in developing economic understanding for students at this grade level is the ability of the teacher

---

[2] Prudence Parker, "Junior High Students Study Early American Economy," *Newsletter* (Joint Council on Economic Education, May, 1963), p. 6.

to recognize the opportunities and understand the economic concepts that are involved.

Grade 9. Civics, or the study of the community, provides the focus. This study usually encompasses a knowledge of the political and economic structure and organization of the community. But where properly taught, this material is related to the various aspects of the individual's life and well-being. Included may be:

The individual as a consumer. Students at this age are a significant part of the consumer market and will become more so in the years ahead. They are participating members of the economy with sizeable discretionary purchasing power. They should understand the importance of the consumer vote and its effect on directing the economy. The relation is clear to the effect they have on production and the direction of investment and many case studies could be developed to illustrate such concepts. A project which begins with checking the reasons for a decline in coffee consumption with a sharp increase in price or the effect on the price of orange juice following a winter freeze in Florida and Wisconsin are illustrations of this. How advertising affects this relationship can be explored. For this unit the nature of wants, consumer sovereignty, income-expenditure data with emphasis on food and durable goods expenditure are excellent areas of study.

The individual as a worker. Many students do have employment experience. This should be related to the production and productivity picture. The student should see himself as part of a team necessitating adjustment to others to bring about the maximum contribution possible for himself and the group of which he is a member. Such a study easily leads to a consideration of the factors involved in the distribution of income.

The individual as a citizen. This is the recognition that one must be an economic as well as a political citizen. The interrelationships among the farm problem, labor problem, urban redevelopment, and fiscal responsibility can be treated as parts of a citizen's concern.

The individual in his relationship to the earth. Here there is the fine opportunity to develop again the basic economic problem of scarcity. Wants and resources available have to be kept in balance, yet the standard of living must improve.

The individual in his relationship to the life and the culture of people of different lands. The economics involved in the work going on with the underdeveloped countries can be introduced. The effect of the level of living of other countries on that of this country can be explored profitably. The population explosion and its effect on standards of living can be illustrated through a study of Brazil or India.

World trade. The opportunity is present to show the effect of world trade on the individual, his community, and the state. A study of the income generated in the community from world trade would be an excellent survey as an introduction to the market system.

The teacher has a responsibility for providing the individual students, especially at this age, with the opportunity of seeing himself in his economic world. This is the time when the highest drop-out occurs in schools. Relating the individual to his economic world provides a different perspective on education, and economic study can have a salient effect on the holding power of the school. Further appropriate comments will be included under the business education section.

Grade 10—World history. The following topics are areas where understandings can be developed.

Economic growth and development. This theme runs throughout history. Capital formation existed in every society, and technological and intellectual advances in knowledge can be recognized as economic factors. Developing an understanding of how savings affects capital formation and the ways of saving that were developed from primitive societies can be accomplished. Tool-making, scientific improvement and knowledge accumulation provide a background for considering why some societies grew faster than others. The relationship can be established between rate of growth and capital accumulation and technological advance.

Comparative economic systems. Every society, whether treated chronologically or through area studies, permits this comparison of economic systems. Every society has faced the problem of scarcity. Every society has had to organize to cope with scarcity. Every society has had to concern itself with what and how, how much, and for whom in making economic decisions.

The allocation of resources is common to all economic societies; individual economic incentives always operate; ownership or private property is lodged somewhere; capital resources and economic growth are ever present; stability requires planning; standard of living is an ever-present concern. The means of achieving these objectives do differ and this makes the comparative approach essential. Varying degrees of economic control within societies do exist but this does not eliminate a democratic political system. Perhaps the greatest differences in societies can be found in their political and social organization rather than in their economic organization.

International trade.   Many insights and concepts in economics can be developed through this topic. Specialization, bilateral and multilateral trade, regional specialization, interdependence, motivations, restrictions to trade, protectionism, gold flow, and free trade are fruitful areas of investigation. Marco Polo, the Phoenicians, the Roman Empire, the Crusades, the development of the British Empire, and colonialism are illustrative of points where, in the stream of history, an emphasis might be given.

Grade 11—American history.   There are several dominant themes that run through a course in United States history. Schools may use a chronological or topical treatment or a combination of both. There is no evidence on hand to prove the superiority of any one of these. Other approaches might deal with developing the turning points in American history, utilizing a series of period history treatments, or viewing the national scene through a variety of autobiographical or biographical studies. But whichever approach is used, the political, economic, and social developments in this country were the outgrowth of efforts of citizens to solve the problems they faced.

Since this course is universal in the American high school and required of all students, several avenues of developing economic understanding would be useful.

Wass suggests that the approach should be through a study of the social goals or themes: economic growth, freedom, stability, security, and justice.[3] Americans have strived to achieve these goals in improving their life situations. The settling of the colonies, the westward movement, and industrial expansion are points where such studies of growth can be made. The era between the Civil War and 1900 is another. But wherever one breaks into the historical scene to develop economic understandings of growth, he will have to con-

---

[3] Philmore B. Wass, "A Major Goal for The High School," *Teacher Education Quarterly,* Vol. XIX, No. 3 (Spring, 1962).

sider the effect of, (1) natural, human, capital, and entrepreneurial resources, (2) institutions developed to foster the attainment of the goals, government contributions via legislation and purchasing power, (3) technological advances, (4) capital accretion, (5) cultural environment, and (6) the market development.

Calderwood recognizes the essential difference between the discipline of economics and that of history. The analytical approach of the economist differs considerably from the process approach of history. Economic information must be viewed as an "orderly and meaningful pattern of systematic relationships."[4] Economics operates from basic assumptions developed within a logical framework to produce a model. Deductions can then be made from these models in facing up to future economic problems by approaching and analyzing these through a disciplined approach. History deals with constant change and rests upon narrative and induction. To integrate these two disciplines may not be possible. But there are convenient points in a historical approach where the events discussed provide a springboard for developing an economic concept of lasting value.

Dominant themes which appear in history and lend themselves to economic analysis are the market systems of decision-making, economic growth, and stability. Each of these can be treated well and will involve the role of business, government and the changing international picture.

The Harvard-Newton project develops economic concepts within the historical framework of case studies of major business corporations but the themes remain the same.[5]

Others would take as the one dominant theme, "Technological Change." Units on the impact of technology on agriculture, the westward movement, manufacturing, transportation and communication, war, labor-management relations, cities and suburbia, money and credit, business organization, international trade, economic freedom and justice, managerial operations, and competition are possible. Certainly it fits the theme of "Growth and Development." It would also be possible to use the chronological approach

---

[4] James Calderwood, *Economic Themes in United States History* (Riverside, Calif.: Office of Riverside County Superintendent of Schools, 1962), p. 1.

[5] Ralph W. Hidy and Paul E. Cawein, *Casebook in Business History and Economic Concepts for Use in Secondary Schools* (Newton, Mass.: Newton Public Schools, 1963).

in reverse and raise the question, "How did things get to be the way they are?" Starting with Chapter 30 and working back to Chapter 1 might be a more interesting approach.

A series of pamphlets on American history produced by Curriculum Resources, Inc., offers a slightly different approach.[6] Here we see an effort made to integrate economics into the chronological development and narrative of America.

There are other approaches and all that can be said is that no one approach has proved itself superior to any other. What is of importance is that the opportunities are abundant to develop important economic understandings in the history course, improving its context and adding a new and important dimension to a study of the American scene.

Grade 12—Problems of democracy or an economics course. The first course referred to familiarly as "P.O.D." is a combination of economic, social, and political dimensions. It offers unparalleled opportunity to develop critical thinking through considering such topics as: economic growth, the farm problem, methods of organizing economic activity in the United States and the Soviet Union, the labor problem, the role of collective bargaining, United States foreign trade policy, changes in the structure of employment, taxation, the role of profits in the U.S., and the free-enterprise economy, a price-directed economic system.

Many others could be added and possibly the best series produced to assist the "P.O.D." teacher in developing economic units is the *Economic Topics* of the Joint Council.[7]

The emphasis on a separate economics course in the high school is perhaps the fastest growing phenomena in the social studies curriculum. There are many excellent guides now available for such a course thereby permitting any school to find a pattern which is compatible to the teacher, the school, and the community. It should be emphasized that this course should not be a watered down version of an introductory college course. These have not succeeded in stimulating the interest of the general student body. Also, such a course should be viewed as a capstone to a sequential approach to economic understanding which starts at Grade 1. Considerable competence is

---

[6] *Economic Forces in American History* (Chicago: Scott, Foresman & Co., 1963).

[7] *Economic Topics, op. cit.*

required of the teacher beyond what is needed at any other grade level or course.

Course outlines in economics have been developed by the University of Illinois Laboratory High School,[8] Pennsylvania State Department of Education,[9] and New York State Department of Education.[10]

The course can be organized around economic problems, principles, consumer economics, or the social goals themes. Whatever approach is used, the emphasis should be upon analysis. Here the student should learn that economics is a way of thinking and whatever approach is used should belabor this point.

General business course. This course is usually offered at the ninth- and tenth-grade level and offers, in its emphasis on economics, an opportunity that must not be bypassed. Most of the students enrolled in this course are not college bound, and are looking forward to some sort of occupation within the offices of a business or manufacturing establishment. Giving these students a good basic background in economics at the beginning of their specialization provides a seriousness of purpose and a means of self-evaluation.

The focus of much of what is done in this course is on personal economics, individual management of his own affairs. The recognition that economics is a social science is, however, taking hold and the student is being prepared to recognize the relationship and the differences between what an individual may do and what the body politic does. Analysis is being stressed. Aggregate economics is becoming the point of departure, leading to the economics of the firm.

Recommendations have been made, and experiments in the classroom have confirmed, that the introductory unit of a course should be an overview of the American economy. Since this is a year's course, a slower pace can be set allowing more time for depth in analysis. A discussion of the wants-scarcity problem can move into how the economy is organized to put into effect decisions that are made. This leads to the market and price system and the choice-

---

[8] Ella C. Leppert and Lewis E. Wagner, "The High School Economics Course: A Suggested Outline" (New York: Joint Council on Economic Education, 1962).

[9] *Suggested Procedures and Resources For A Minimum Course in Economics,* Curriculum Development Series No. 4 (Harrisburg, Pa.: Department of Public Instruction, Commonwealth of Pennsylvania, 1962).

[10] *American History and Economics,* Curriculum Bulletin No. 10, 1961–62 Series (New York: Board of Education, City of New York, 1962).

making process of society. Costs in an economic sense can be discussed as they are applied to the individual, to businesses, to government units, to national allocations of capital, and to international activities. The above can be related to the considerations of growth and stability as well as the other goals of the economy and the interrelationships explored.

A section of the course should deal with the consumer's role as well. Campbell outlines this, covering the nature of wants, consumer sovereignty through the production process, and the stimulation of demand.[11] Covered also should be the income-expenditure data which relates to the national income accounts and moves into the total process of analysis as defined by the Task Force.

Moving from this base to that which is more applicable to the business firm, units on the role of the producer, business organization, bigness and efficiency, research and development, aggregate business indicators and their relationship to the health of the economy, and income distribution within a business and financing expansion of operations can be introduced. Monetary and fiscal policy should be examined and applied to the operation of a business. The function of credit and its relation with savings and investment can be explored. The shared risk concept is applicable to business operation and individual security. And of importance is the relationship of business operation today to the role of the government.

Other business education courses. Stenography and typing opportunities were described in the first chapter.

Bookkeeping—Through a study of the accounting procedure, a deeper understanding of profits can be developed. The attention given to the "T accounts" is important here and the problem of developing operating budgets can be related to that of the National Budget. National Income Accounting can be developed in depth. The keeping of international accounts is also important, leading to an understanding of international trade, investment, aid, and the problems connected with them.

Business law—Business law can develop a better understanding of the terminology used in daily life, such as credit, private property, economic rights, legalities of corporations, the utilization of pension funds and other accumulations of capital. The legal pro-

---

[11] Persia Campbell, "The Consumer Approach," *Economics in General Education* (New York: Joint Council on Economic Education, 1954), p. 117.

tections afforded by the government through laws can be examined from the aspect of correcting abuses.

There are other courses in this area of the high school curriculum and studies have detailed the economics that can be taught within their structure.

Other secondary school courses. A brief word will suffice to point out the opportunities of introducing economics in courses which will stimulate the interest of the student.

Mathematics, for example, includes a knowledge of statistics, employment theory, use of graphs (time series data), and finance. Problems can be developed around any area of economic analysis, and the financial records of the local community can be used to provide realistic data.

Students in literature classes will develop a deeper appreciation of the books being read if they understand the economy out of which the literature developed. The purpose of such a study is to develop a greater appreciation of the literature.

In science courses, too, the isolation of the science breaks down where the economic applications of technological advances are discussed.

Home economics presents the teacher with the opportunity of relating the economy of the family unit to that of the nation. The consumer approach described earlier can yield dividends. Savings and the relationship of various kinds of savings flowing through the institutions into the economy for capital expansion purposes can be more easily understood.

The opportunities in the curriculum are boundless. The advantages can be easily recognized. But the crux of the entire problem of developing economic literacy is the background of the teacher. This is still the solution to the problem and it must be sought on our college campuses to a greater extent.

CHAPTER VII

The Responsibility of Colleges and Universities for Economic Education

The responsibility of institutions of higher learning in this area of knowledge is important but perhaps no greater or less than that for any other area of knowledge. There are adherents for the other disciplines equally as insistent in their claims as those in economics. In this writer's opinion, the problem of collegiate responsibility stems from the fact that the various divisions existing on a campus have generally isolated themselves from one another. In these days of specialization, the chemist sees little of the professors in the allied sciences. The political scientist has little contact with the economist, the economist with the sociologist, and so on through the other disciplines.

This dissociation has been even more pronounced in the relationship between other divisions on the campus and education. The Liberal Arts Division has assumed little responsibility for the preparation of teachers for elementary, secondary, and even collegiate teaching. So little understanding existed among the defenders of the liberal arts that this refusal to participate in teacher preparation was tantamount to weakening the very means to a continuing high calibre of the inheritors of liberal arts teaching. Knowledge can only be nurtured and improved if those who are to teach it are capable of the effort. The transmission of knowledge is only as good as the transmitter.

Experiences in the classroom, such as those described above, are dependent to a great extent on the assistance that is available from a continuing relationship between the lower schools and a university or college.

Teachers cannot be expected to be aware of, or informed about, all of the aspects of the subject they are teaching or of the methods designed to produce the best results. Keeping the curriculum up to date requires a continuing relationship between the scholars and the teachers. Knowledge is changing rapidly, and research in student capacity and learning technique requires the teacher to refresh himself constantly.

There is little question that the responsibility for the lack of economic education in the schools can be laid at the doorstep of those who prepare the teachers. The deficiencies of the teachers are simply the deficiencies of their college professors, then communicated to elementary and secondary students through the teacher as an intermediary. Teacher-preparation institutions, and this includes the liberal arts colleges which still provide a large percentage of the secondary school teachers, are not developing teachers capable of meeting the new demands of society. New methods are needed, but it took a sputnik to bring about the self-evaluation of the American educational system that had been so long overdue.

Recent years, however, have seen a very promising movement. The schools, the community, and the university are joining forces in a way that is bringing improvements. Gains have become evident for all of the parties concerned. Contact with the schools and the teachers have given the professors that face-to-face reality of the classroom from which they had been isolated. Observing the procedures in the schools forced the professors into a self-evaluation of the teaching techniques used in the collegiate classroom and improvements followed. Universities possessed the resources that could be of major assistance in producing a better equipped and more confident teacher, and this task is now given a high priority.

When one turns to economics and the university's responsibility for improving economic literacy for all citizens through the medium of the classroom, the problem of teacher preparation becomes paramount. The knowledge of the techniques and procedures which can be utilized in developing the competent teacher is available, perhaps, to a much greater degree than their actual demonstration by the professor in the classroom. Objectives, selection of content, classroom aids of an audio or visual nature, a variety of methods and materials, a utilization of community resources, and an effective evaluation program are salient parts of the process. Each professor must individualize his own teaching, for effectiveness in the classroom is an individual thing. Such self-evaluation will have to be carried on to determine the techniques which best suit the teacher. But this will take constant effort and experimentation in the classroom. This is the message which should be left with every future teacher but not by words alone; only by example and practice can the best learning take place.

The final result of all education is developing in the student the ability "to go it alone." This process or technique can be started at the early stages of formal education, but future teachers must experience such methods in the college classroom. Schools must provide the best environment for learning how to go about researching a problem, answering a question, or satisfying a particular curiosity. The student should feel impelled to pursue the knowledge he needs to permit a satisfying and intelligent answer. When learning challenges the imagination, imaginative classroom procedures are likely to follow.

At Syracuse University in 1955–56, an effort was made to develop procedures for future teachers in an experimental course in economic education that would develop a desire for student investigation.[1] The course was for six semester credits and was offered to junior and senior social studies majors in the School of Education. "The main objectives of this particular experiment [were]: 1. to determine whether an adequate group of analytical essentials can be developed as an adjunct to the problem-solving approach to economics (without a formally organized presentation of the theoretical framework); 2. to test the merits and pitfalls of placing in the hands of the students themselves a major share of the responsibility for the organization of the course, the selection of content, and the choice of procedures."

At the first session the general objectives of the course were outlined. The students were invited to assume the major role in determining procedures. Motivation was thus stimulated since the course was their own. The teacher-dominated classroom was a contrast. Euthusiasm was sustained, and group morale was high.

Starting from student interest, three problems in economics were tackled each semester. The areas covered were (1) organization of business and the monetary, banking, and financial system, (2) labor organization, labor relations, collective bargaining, and labor legislation, (3) the farm problem, and (4) the general problem of

---

[1] Archibald M. McIsaac, *Interim Report on Experimental Course in Economic Education at Syracuse University, 1955–56* (New York: Joint Council on Economic Education, 1956).

economic growth and stability. The final two weeks of the course were devoted to tying together the various themes studied during the year.

The professor served as a resource person and avoided lectures. Some readings were assigned, and other were suggested. A text was used. Approaches used included the class acting as a committee of the whole with individual responsibilities assigned by the group. One unit was tackled by five separate committees investigating different phases of the problem. Outside speakers were brought in, and panels organized for presentations. In a later unit on growth and stability, "several subcommittees were elected to study rather diverse fields with a special eye to their relations to the general problem."[2] A wide variety of materials was available in the classroom. Newspapers and magazines provided the current information, charts and other visual aids were student-prepared. Films and filmstrips were used.

The class did their own evaluation of the course and assisted in evaluating their own performance. Criteria for individual evaluations were established, and student conferences with the professor produced an agreement on grades. "The general level of performance was, we thought, better than we had commonly encountered in the conventionally conducted course."[3] A group responsibility was generated and the confidence placed in the students was reflected in their accomplishments. Self-criticism was plentiful but expressed constructively.

There was still some doubt of whether as much of a grasp of the analytical tools was attained as would have been through the conventional course. Analysis brought in piecemeal still had to be measured against the systematic approach. But these new problems provided a point of attack for the next year's course.

Other notable examples of good teaching can be found at Oklahoma State University, Washington University, University of Iowa, Purdue, Ohio State, Illinois, Southern Connecticut State, and Wellesley.

The characteristics found in all of these classroms include, first, the freedom given the student to investigate. This is learning by doing. The resulting familiarity with the method developed in such

---

2 *Ibid.*, p. 3.
3 *Ibid.*, p. 4.

teacher-preparation programs will find its transference later to the elementary and the secondary students. The steps in economic analysis and the problems approach are practiced, and failure as well as success is experienced. Analysis does not come about only by reading. The process provides a goal toward which the student sets his course. The sooner the potential teacher is introduced to the wonders of and necessity for such research the stronger will be the desire to introduce future students to the research technique however elementary it may be. Self-reliance and an intellectual freedom can thus be promoted.

Second, the utilization of a variety of experiences inside or outside the classroom provides a broader approach to learning than the narrow limits of the traditional course. The varying abilities of the students can be fully discovered and extended through these activities, thus approaching a condition that more nearly provides a sense of achievement for all students.

Third, the pattern of any curriculum that emphasizes individual responsibility in achieving proficiency in any course, and the one that places its faith on individuals developing the ability for independent investigation is the one that offers the best hope for education. The "problems approach," the emphasis on the development of concepts, and the utilization of the economics laboratory are contributory factors to the development of good teachers. These characteristics will develop the intellectual freedom and responsibility that the educational process demands.

Metcalf has emphasized the deficiencies in teacher preparation in the social studies by his comments on the practice of teachers in "inculcating right answers, right attitudes, right beliefs. The process of teaching in the closed areas is an amalgam of suppression, indoctrination, distortion, manipulation, prescription, and persuasion."[4] This is called brainwashing if done in Iron Curtain countries.

"In place of charlatanism and incantation we need an honestly reflective study of contrasting ideologies with no suppression of knowledge as its intent or by-product. This kind of teaching would preserve that part of our cultural heritage which merits survival, and would build the only kind of patriotism compatible with democratic

---

[4] Lawrence E. Metcalf, "Some Guidelines for Changing Social Studies Education," *Social Education* (April, 1963), p. 197.

values."[5] Metcalf further stresses the need for better motivation in preparing teachers in economics. Relevance of material and knowledge to current issues provides meaning for the student. Problem-solving gives purpose to economics. Analysis needs to be emphasized in the methods courses, but methods courses must be built around content in learning how to apply this knowledge to classroom instruction.

The responsibilities of institutions preparing future teachers in economics are outlined below.

1. *Major requirements of course of study.* The requirements of the college or university for social studies and business education teaching majors should be carefully reviewed. In the former group a balance of social science courses should be instituted with a minimum of six semester hours in economics. A minor in economics should be offered in addition, permitting students to complete up to 18 semester hours of work if they desire.

The endless argument between the state certifying authorities and the teacher-preparation institutions should be brought to conclusion. The focus for the decisions should be on the qualifications which schools need in the teachers they employ. The colleges have a responsibility for preparing the students for the market place (the school systems) or they are not fulfilling their obligations.

Kentucky has attacked the balance of teacher preparation in a unique way, one that could serve as an example well worth following. There, secondary teachers, in order to be certified in the social studies, must have "a minimum of 48 semester hours distributed as follows: 18 semester hours of history . . . 30 semester hours selected from political science, economics, sociology and geography . . . with a minimum of six semester hours in each and with a maximum of twelve semester hours in any one of these subjects."[6] This requirement of at least a minimum of six semester hours in each of the social sciences specified provides for a balanced program of teacher preparation; the maximum of twelve hours provides for a greater degree of depth and flexibility.

2. *Interdepartmental Coordination.* The preparation of future

---

[5] *Ibid.,* p. 198.

[6] "Guidelines for Programs of Teacher Preparation Certification," *Educational Bulletin,* Vol. XXX, No. 1, (Frankfort, Kentucky: Board of Education, January, 1962), 66.

teachers and the providing of in-service opportunities for teachers to eliminate deficiencies in their backgrounds of knowledge and method must be a responsibility assumed by colleges and universities. No longer can the liberal arts departments and the schools and departments of education abrogate their obligations. A joint approach, both in planning the programs and executing them, must be developed. Economic education, by its very definition, necessitates such cooperation on the campus. At least one person on the faculty should be assigned to give special attention to coordinating the university functions. His work would be in the area of teacher preparation within and outside the university. A person with a dual professorship in economics and education would be ideal, but these people are still to be developed and accorded the full rights and privileges of any other member of the faculty.

3. *Off-campus activities.* Modern teaching in the United States requires that every school system maintain a close relationship between its faculty and the faculties of nearby colleges and universities. Constant consultation should be carried on by the professors in economics with the teachers in the schools. Assistance can be offered in evaluating materials and producing those which have regional and local significance. Bureaus of business research have valuable economic information which awaits interpretation and communication to the students at many grade levels.

In-service economic education programs should be offered to the faculties of the schools. These can be conducted either with or without course credit through weekly seminars, institutes, lecture-discussion series or workshops. Maximum use should be made of all of the educational tools available, and departments in the school of education can be enlisted to provide and produce kinescopes of TV programs, films and filmstrips, charts and graphs.

Student teaching deserves even greater attention than it is now getting, and this is a shared responsibility of both the economics department and the school of education. No longer should a student preparing himself for the profession feel that his content background has been developed on one part of the campus, the methods on another part, and "never the twain shall meet." Rather, since his preparatory work should be done jointly, his practice teaching should be coordinated also. Secondary social studies teachers, competent in the field of economics, should be selected to supervise the prospective teacher. Close contact and constant refresher courses should be given these supervisory people. They can be groomed to serve as school consultants in this manner. By the same token, the economist will be forced to keep up to date, not only in his own field, but also in learning theory and techniques. The professor of education would have to become equally as competent in the discipline of economics as the economist would be in education. Practice teaching of this sort would come right after, or concomitant with, course instruction on the campus. This would insure the maximum retention of the knowledge and fortify the techniques of presentation acquired.

4. *Curriculum Library*. Somewhere on the campus a complete library of economic education materials should be available. Purdue University and the University of Illinois have developed laboratories for economic education within the departments of economics. Classes for future teachers in economics are carried on in these laboratories replete with samples of student materials, pamphlets of a "fugitive" nature, films, filmstrips, teachers guides, and other teaching aids. The materials center at Eastern Michigan University provides materials to the surrounding schools. At San Diego County, California, school headquarters a complete library service is maintained with the cooperation and assistance of San Diego State College.

5. *Graduate Programs in Economic Education*. Meeting the demand for persons competently prepared to teach economics is crucial to achieving success. Collegiate institutions will have to give consideration to establishing programs that adequately prepare a candidate in the discipline, yet at the same time permit him to acquire competence in teaching. Master's and doctoral programs have been established in several universities, notably Illinois, Iowa, Purdue, and Minnesota. Again interdepartmental cooperation will be required. An M.A. or Ph.D. program in economic education should be no less rigorous than one in economics and perhaps even more exacting. Difficult questions such as how much mathematical economics will be required, or will theses related to this area of education be accepted need to be answered.

Another factor that negates work being done by teachers in the area of economics is the reluctance and refusal of economic departments to establish an introductory course in economics which will carry graduate credit. Teachers are constantly working for their advanced degrees, and, because of the certification requirements, faulty information received from an advisor assigned by the college, or personal decisions, deficiencies in background exist. Such adjustments do not do any harm to the program for majors in economics. Social studies teachers are expected to have a proficiency in a variety of fields which precludes, at the undergraduate level, basic work in all of the social science disciplines. Present rules and regulations on the campus must be reexamined in the light of the needs.

6. *Research*. The parochialism of thinking in reference to what constitutes research needs to be reexamined. The evaluation of what is now going on in the name of research is best left to the scholars of the field but a fresh look needs to be given to the kind and type of research now needed. More detailed information to this area of study will be given in the next chapter, but suffice it to say here, that advancing the cause of economic literacy requires a type of research not now recognized as being important by the economist. Present research is directed more toward answering the question of, "Economics for what?"

7. *Service*. Aside from the direct work with and services to the teachers, the university has a distinct responsibility to the community in creating an environment for the development of economic education. There are many informational and promotional activities to be carried on. The people of any given area should have a point of contact when seeking information relating to economics. The liaison among persons, organizations, and institutions professionally concerned with economics could well be assumed by the school. And along with this goes the necessary reporting of activities whether in research, in professional achievement, or among the groups whose cooperation is needed in developing a successful program.

> "Although the service aspects of a program in economic education are unlikely to yield the immediate, tangible results of other facets of the program, the importance of this function should not be underestimated. Service activities kindle interest and provide individuals with information on problems, programs, and ways in which they may participate. The cumulative effect of service activities can, in only a relatively short time, generate a variety of programs throughout the state."[7]

---

[7] Lewis E. Wagner, *Report of Progress In Economic Education* (Urbana, Illinois: University of Illinois, Nov. 19, 1958), p. 13.

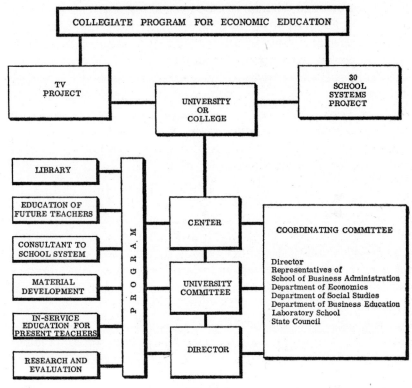

Figure 2

Centers of Economic Education are conducted in several universities as follows:

Boston University, Boston, Massachusetts
Brigham Young University, Provo, Utah
Colorado State College of Education, Greeley, Colorado
Georgia State College, Atlanta, Georgia
Montclair State College, Upper Montclair, New Jersey
Ohio University, Athens, Ohio
Oklahoma State University, Stillwater, Oklahoma
Pomona College, Claremont, California
Purdue University, Lafayette, Indiana
San Francisco State College, San Francisco, California
Southern Connecticut State College, New Haven, Connecticut
State University of Iowa, Iowa City, Iowa
University of Connecticut, Storrs, Connecticut
University of Illinois, Champaign, Illinois
University of Minnesota, Minneapolis, Minnesota

University of Wisconsin, Milwaukee, Wisconsin
Utah State University, Logan, Utah
Texas Technological College, Lubbock, Texas

A viable means for universities and colleges to accomplish the results implied in the responsibilities listed above has been developing since 1959. These efforts were reported in the publication of the Joint Council on Economic Education entitled, *A Developing Program of Centers of Economic Education.*[8] (See Fig. 2 *Collegiate Program for Economic Education*)

The conceptual framework for the organization of such a center in no way represents that existing on any campus today. It merely illustrates the variety of functions that can be performed and the administrative relationship. Each of the 18 centers listed are carrying on many of the functions which will be summarized below, but all are seeking with each additional year's activities to strengthen their programs.

Functions of Collegiate Centers

1. *Undergraduate and graduate courses in economics and economic education.* The introductory course and a modification of the principles course, economic history, labor economics, money and banking, public finance, alternative economic systems, and economic geography constitute a range of courses which have a close relationship to the school curriculum. At the graduate level, courses, such as contemporary economic problems, comparative systems, the economics of industry, international economic problems, industrial development of a particular state or region, and economic growth, continue in depth the work at the undergraduate level.

Obviously each institution will determine what courses its faculty members think most adequately prepare the teacher of the elementary and secondary school. Faculties would also be wise to consider what would be most beneficial for those who will be teaching at the junior college level, as well. Courses in theory will be a continuing requirement, but they need not become an "either/or" proposition. Clark Bloom, at the State University of Iowa, in the introductory courses, reserves a portion of the time at the end of each course for

---

[8] *A Developing Program of Centers of Economic Education* (New York: Report to the Board of Trustees of the Joint Council on Economic Education, November, 1960).

student analysis of a variety of policy statements. Such critical reviews gave purpose to the theory. Oklahoma State places its emphasis on an interpretation of the theory into some phase of the school program related directly to the work of the teacher taking the course.

The establishment of programs leading to advanced degrees has become formalized at several institutions, but a program can be planned at any one of the centers which would, in effect, be comparable to advanced degree programs now in operation.

2. *Conferences and workshops which the colleges or universities help to organize and conduct.* Such programs are developed, in the main, for teachers in-service. Montclair State College in New Jersey provided such programs for over a thousand teachers in 1963. Pomona College Center in California conducted a seminar for teachers representing nine school districts in the area. Graduate credit was offered, but to qualify for such credit the teacher participants had to submit detailed original comprehensive curriculum plans for use in the social studies curriculums of their respective schools. The staff at Pomona also assisted the Temple City, California, schools to develop an ambitious program designed to provide students in Grade 9–12 with an integrated work experience and an economic education curriculum revolving around these experiences. *Economic Education in Taylorville* details the approach used by the University of Illinois.[9]

Another type of conference has been sponsored by these Centers with the assistance of their associated council on economic education. These are the state conferences for collegiate economists, deans, and professors of education from institutions throughout the state. These centers have been concerned with reproducing their services in a number of areas to bring the assistance needed directly to the schools in local areas. Orientation, organization, program problems, and research have been discussed. Close association with other campuses is sought and consultation offered.

3. *College centers also emphasize research, publications, and distribution and development of instructional materials in their comprehensive program.* Consultant services of the center should be made available to the schools. Schools need assistance in developing

---

[9] *Economic Education in Taylorville* (Taylorville, Illinois: Taylorville Community Unit School, 1959).

research designs and evaluation techniques. Sufficient graduate assistants should be available to provide the manpower needed in gathering the information and following through with the other work needed. Many state departments of education are seeking this sort of competence for projects they are conducting. School systems, through their curriculum or research offices, would welcome assistance from those expert in the field. The Joint Council and many other national groups are looking for centers of strength to carry out investigation and research in areas affecting the development of programs in economic education. Centers must act on the assumption that in order to be effective, school programs in economic education require a knowledge of research findings in curriculum content and student achievement.

Centers have produced many publications that have made fine contributions to economic education. The special economic education issues of the Illinois *Councilor*[10] and of the Connecticut *Teacher Education Quarterly*,[11] the publications on the experimental elementary school program developed at Purdue University and Elkhart, Indiana,[12] the Comparative Economies Filmstrip in the Laboratory School at the University of Illinois,[13] the numerous teacher guides developed at Brigham Young University, and the special edition of the *Iowa Business Digest*[14] are samples. Bibliographies, special monographs, and articles prepared for national publications are the result of activities of centers. The Iowa *Primers*[15] are a notable example of center-prepared student materials. At San Francisco, the center has cooperated with the Joint Council in preparing the syllabus for a high school economics course.

Service bulletins are published by some centers periodically. New materials are described, resources and experiences reported on, and special programs announced.

A materials center is another important focus for the work. Each center should offer perhaps the largest collection of sources and aids

[10] *The Councilor* (March, 1960), *op. cit.*
[11] "Economic Education," *Teacher Education Quarterly*, Vol. XIX, No. 3 (Spring, 1962).
[12] Senesh, *My Home, Curriculum Guide Social Studies Grade One, op. cit.*
[13] *Methods of Organizing Economic Activity* (Urbana, Illinois: University High School, 1959).
[14] *Iowa Business Digest* (Winter, 1957).
[15] "Primers" (Iowa City: Bureau of Business and Economic Research, College of Business Administration, State University of Iowa).

in economic education anywhere in the state. Through an organized relationship, councils and centers all over the country exchange information and materials. The Joint Council on Economic Education also services these centers with a steady flow of source items. Those organizations cooperating with the Joint Council through arrangement, also forward their materials directly to such centers. As a result one of the most important services to the schools is provided. There is a constant evaluation by the centers of new materials thus enabling schools and teachers to separate the usable items from those with little validity or usability. Sample kits of materials or kits of resources available for any curriculum study are sent out on request.

4. *Continuing consultant services are available to schools, communities, and organizations of various types from some centers.* Special studies can be undertaken for course development. Economists are necessary for any curriculum revision which is to take place and campus advisory service is made available to any student.

Many schools today are undertaking total revision of the social studies and business education curriculums. Centers are in the unique position to provide the resources needed in economics. Personnel from the centers will find themselves appointed to commissions established by the State Board of Education or other governmental agencies, state professional organizations, and business and labor organizations. The demand is great for those who have made a specialty of economic education.

The activities of the center in Illinois serving as a consultant initiator and developer illustrate the variety of activities engaged in over a two-year period:[16]

. . . Fifteen conferences and workshops which the university helped organize and conduct.

. . . Faculty members attended and delivered papers at 22 conferences in ten different states. These were for educational, professional, farm, and business groups.

. . . Organized six in-service programs attended by 150 teachers responsible for economic education in four school systems.

. . . Experimented with special sections of the introductory course for those preparing to teach. Total enrollment was 130 students.

. . . Developed and taught twice the experimental high school course in economics at the Laboratory school for 50 students.

---

[16] Wagner, *Report of Progress in Economic Education, op. cit.*

... Contributed over 14 articles or monographs on economic education.

... Served as a member of nine state or national committees or boards in addition to carrying on correspondence on projects with a variety of schools in and out of the state.

... Stimulated the graduate programs in economic education at the University.

Administratively, the centers exemplify one of Conant's strong recommendations of an all-university responsibility for teacher preparation.[17] A campus-wide committee is a necessity and consists of representatives from economics, business education, social studies education, the laboratory school, bureaus of business and educational research, and any other division of the university that can make a contribution to economic education. In the past, the center has either been part of a division of the School of Education or Business Administration, or lodged in the Department of Economics. A strong recommendation, resulting from the experience thus far, is made for the center to be constituted as an administrative division responsible directly to a dean yet continuing to operate with an all-university committee as its board. The director should be a person of senior professorial rank and his table or organization should include both those expert in professional curriculum planning and subject-matter knowledge. Sufficient graduate assistants and secretarial help should be available to carry out the work. The center should operate on an independent budget, similar to any other department within the university.

Obviously, there will be a number of patterns developed for the establishment of such centers. Conditions differ within institutions. Demands in some states are farther advanced than others. Private institutions may be limited in their ability to commit budgets to a greater extent than those institutions whose budgets include services to the citizens of the state. Councils on economic education will vary in strength, and their ability to provide additional resources to the centers for specific services will be limited.

But the fact remains that if the people of the United States want an economically literate citizenry, then it will have to provide a mechanism such as described here. A continuing program estab-

---

17 James B. Conant, *The Education of American Teachers* (New York: McGraw-Hill Book Company, 1963).

lished at the basic source of good education, teacher preparation, must be established operating both on and off campus. Dealing in the area so sensitive to community pressures precludes any one "right way" or "one set of materials." There will be diversity within a broad framework of what the goal may be, whether it be that described by the Task Force or that developed by some other group. The approach must be kept open-ended, because economics or any social science and behavioral science is in constant change. Truths are merely working hypotheses. How true this is in economic education is detailed by the needs for research.

CHAPTER VIII

Research and Evaluation Needs

Education has long been deficient in the areas of research and evaluation. It is as though this deficiency has almost been planned. Teacher preparation has paid scant attention to the need for objectively determining whether or not the aims stated for a curriculum or a course or a grade-level program were actually being achieved. The philosophers have left their mark on teaching procedures, but there has been little research to indicate whether these new techniques were an improvement over those which had been replaced. Claims based on a subjective judgment of teachers, administrators, parents, employers, or students sufficed to determine whether or not success had been achieved.

In recent years, however, there has been a steady accumulation of data. Each new advance, in itself, has contributed little, but as available information has increased, many myths and prejudices have been revealed. Developments of late in the exact sciences and electronic technology, plus the temper of the times in an era of exploding educational costs, have brought demands that education prove its claims.

Economics, as one of the social sciences, is no exception to these demands. The need for economic literacy is widely recognized, and funds have been forthcoming to develop programs that would achieve such literacy. What has been accomplished in the past 15 years has been termed successful by many, but actual research and evaluation programs have not been widely developed as yet.

If proper research and evaluation were to be carried on, however, certain basic studies and reports had to be prepared. The Joint Council on Economic Education, the American Economic Association, and the Committee for Economic Development deserve credit for recognizing this need and joining forces to stimulate the research and evaluation that was, and continues to be, so necessary. The resulting documents serve as guides to content, study materials, textbooks, teaching techniques, and tests.

The report, *Economic Education in the Schools,* presented a professional framework of the minimum requirement in economics needed upon graduation from the twelfth grade to qualify for effective citizenship.[1] Economic education programs were thus given a frame of reference against which to measure the scope of their undertakings. For the first time the content of economics was defined for the schools and the economist's method of analysis explained.

A second report by a Materials Evaluation Committee, on study materials for use in schools, examined the "fugitive" materials available to the schools and developed criteria for teachers to use in selecting items for classroom use.[2] A measure or standard of acceptability was established and the materials, by their very content, helped the teachers to determine what was and was not economics.

A third report, by a selected group of economists, examined the most widely used textbooks in the social studies at the secondary school level. By studying "Economics in the Schools," the teachers were able to see the criteria used for judging the suitability of such texts in achieving economic competence.[3] Evaluation of text material in use in the schools was made possible. Within the report itself, economic analysis and its components were examined and illustrated.

An additional tool was added by the educational television production of a nationwide program "The American Economy."[4] Here was striking proof of the ability to teach economics in an objective, analytical fashion. The confidence of the viewing audience provided the schools with a program that in its entirety was relatively noncontroversial. Techniques of teaching were demonstrated and what appeared to be difficult concepts were explained clearly and simply. A standard of achievement was set for teacher preparation.

A final tool for instituting proper research and evaluation was the *Test of Economic Understanding* developed by a distinguished group for diagnostic use by the schools and colleges.[5] Taking the report of the Task Force as its guide, a standardized testing instrument was made available for the first time to measure content, coverage, understanding of concepts, and achievements. Some measure of evalu-

---

[1] *Economic Education in the Schools, op. cit.*

[2] *Study Materials for Economic Education in the Schools, op. cit.*

[3] "Economics in the Schools," *American Economic Review, op. cit.*

[4] "The American Economy," *op. cit.*

[5] *Test of Economic Understanding* (Chicago: Committee for Measurement of Economic Understanding, Science Research Associates, 1963).

ation is now possible, and further research will refine the present instrument and lead to the development of others. An *Inventory of Economic Understanding,* a check list, is also available to conduct status studies of school programs.[6]

Most economic education programs have developed a set of objectives, and surveys permit summarizing these. The characteristics of the economy and how it operates are basic to understanding. An examination of the persistent problems should be undertaken and the range of alternative solutions examined. Economic education must deal with the major economic institutions and examine the forms of industrial, labor, agricultural, and governmental organization. The role of the market and the place of money exchange within the market need to be examined. This naturally leads to a comprehension of economic growth and stability. Understanding the individual in his role as a producer, consumer, and investor is part of economic literacy. And, finally, the ability to compare economic systems and apply analysis to the world economy are basic requirements to knowledge about, and understanding of, the American economic system. Are these objectives valid? Should others be added or substituted? Arriving at answers to these questions involves a clear understanding of the knowledge and understandings implicit in the study of economics.

Economic relationships need to be understood and the relationship of the parts to the whole discerned. The efficient use of resources should be seen as a part of a rising standard of living. Scarcity and security are recognized as part of the same allocation problem. Growth needs to be recognized as a combination of forces requiring a proper mix. The various sectors of the economy should be observed as a partnership in producing a proper flow of goods and services. The relationship of national economies to other national economies is another area of importance. The interplay of price, supply, and demand should be recognized as an allocation problem. And the effect of economic competence on political responsibility and freedom should be understood.

Necessary skills and abilities would include the ability to define a problem, to determine reliability of data sources, to select the relevant from the irrelevant, to follow through on the process of analysis,

---

[6] *Inventory of Economic Understanding* (New York: Joint Council on Economic Education, 1957).

and distinguish between laws and hypotheses. Stereotypes and myths should be recognized and made to stand the test of fact and evidence. Tradition must be examined for what it is and exposed to the realities of a dynamic economy. Such a summary itself suggests further research. If these are the objectives, then courses of study, materials, techniques, tests, and any other teaching procedures need to be examined to see if they are leading to these objectives or have little relationship to them.

Clark Bloom, and others, in reporting on needed research in economic education identify somewhat the same areas as Wagner.[7] The range of variables is recognized. Enrollments, curricula and courses, materials, methods, teacher certification requirements, interests and abilities of students at various levels, environmental factors, the place of economics in the curriculum, and the nature and role of organizations in economic education outside the schools and colleges are areas where basic knowledge is needed to establish some benchmarks. A good many studies are reported in the literature, but their comprehensiveness is limited.

Areas of profitable research in economic education are many, but Wagner's organization is summarized because of its comprehensiveness.[8]

1. Much information is needed on the current status and practices of economic education in the schools. Because of the lack of uniform understanding of the definition of economics, basic information and data are needed on what is being taught, the scope of the knowledge taught, the grade levels where it is presently being taught, the teaching methods, the competence of economics teachers, the number of students being affected, and the effectiveness of the present programs.

Claims now being made for courses in economics in the schools could well be examined in light of their objectives and in light of their conceptual framework as compared to the Task Force Report. Problems of democracy, history, business education, and home economics courses require similar evaluation. Answers are necessary to questions about reliance on description or analysis. Further studies

[7] Bloom, "Research in Economic Education," *Economics in General Education, op. cit.,* pp. 141–148.

[8] Lewis E. Wagner, *Some Comments on Economic Education as a Subject for Research* (New York: Joint Council on Economic Education, 1957).

of texts are required. The proper combination has yet to be established.

More work is necessary in evaluating the supplementary materials useful to the schools. The work of the Materials Evaluation Committee should be continued and expanded. The gaps in available materials can, through such research, be identified. The criteria for selection can be refined, and guidelines established for those interested in producing materials for use in the schools.

Much more evidence on teacher background and preparation is necessary. How well prepared are the teachers now and what is the practice of the teacher-preparation institutions in insuring adequacy in content and methodological background? Such research is necessary to determine what has yet to be done. Types of in-service programs should be tested in control situations. The amount of economics needed by teachers to teach successfully at the various grade levels still remains a question. This type of information should determine the nature of programs for teacher improvement in economic education.

One further area in need of study is the composition, extent, and practices of economic education groups outside educational institutions who are offering assistance to the schools. A differentiation has to be established between what is education in economics and what is propaganda of a self-seeking nature.

2. A second area of needed research is that which is comparative in nature, seeking to ascertain whether gains have been made in the last 15 years in economic education. Studies both of a qualitative and quantitative nature are needed. Comparisons of textual material would be valuable. The use of materials other than texts needs to be ascertained. Comparisons of economic concepts included in various curricula could perhaps identify trends. An updating of the Brookings Report[9] is long overdue since it represents one of the few benchmarks in economic education in existence. Changes which have occurred in the elementary school should be reflected in the secondary school and then in the colleges and universities. Admitted that the information base for such studies is meager but what is done now could provide some valuable benchmarks ten years from now.

Supplementary studies on teacher certification and requirements

---

[9] C. W. McKee and H. C. Moulton, *A Survey of Economic Education* (Washington, D.C.: The Brookings Institution, 1951).

to those already conducted by the Joint Council would be fruitful. Relating the need for economic education to the social environment would likewise be beneficial in making sound judgments on necessary revisions in teacher preparation and certification.

3. A third area of research is of an experimental or laboratory nature. Concrete evidence must be attained on how much of the content of economics can be successfully taught in a twelve-grade sequence, within the bounds of a balanced curriculum whose objectives are in tune with the modern world. Senesh's[10] work with the Elkhart, Indiana, schools and Taba's[11] work with the Contra Costa, Pleasant Hill, California, schools are examples of this type of research. In Contra Costa the experiment has another dimension of importance, that of ascertaining the capacity of young students for critical thinking in the social studies. Bellack and Davitz in their report, *The Language of the Classroom* developed at the twelfth-grade level and focused on world trade, takes another significant step in providing some pertinent data on classroom teaching in economics.[12]

Rachel Sutton reports on research conducted "to distinguish between process and product in concept formation."[13] Her concern was to collect data on the developmental pattern of economic concepts and determine the nature of this conceptual development as it relates to a social science discipline. She has summarized the research done on the process children follow in concept formation, conceptual learning, and retention through significant experiences. The transfer of retained information for use in tackling new hypotheses is also reported, along with the features in the growth of economic concepts, and the relation of these concepts to the cultural pattern within which the child exists is examined. These studies indicate the directions in which research may go.

Today many subjective judgments are being made on how much of economics students may successfully understand. Much has been made of the differences of ability, but little has been done to relate

---

10 Senesh, *My Home, Curriculum Guide Social Studies Grade One, op. cit.*

11 Hilda Taba, *Social Studies Grades I-VI* (Pleasant Hill, California: Contra Costa County Schools, 1963).

12 Arno A. Bellack and Joel R. Davitz, *The Language of the Classroom* (New York: Teacher's College, Columbia University, 1963).

13 Rachel Sutton, "Behavior in the Attainment of Economic Concepts," *The Journal of Psychology,* Vol. 53 (1962), 37–46.

these differences to economics presented in simplified language and meaningful experiences. The questions of maturity and interests need to be reconciled to achieving understanding in economics. Successful methods, materials, and community involvement may have a bearing on achievement. The curriculum pattern may encourage or discourage achievement. Little, if any, evidence is on hand of this nature that will allow anything but a subjective opinion.

The time for controlled experiments in addition to the more survey-oriented or census-taking types of research has now arrived. What is needed is sufficient evidence that would enable those in the field to state, with some degree of certainty, what economic concepts can be learned by what types of students under what types of conditions. Such information would serve as a base for reconstructing the curriculum, revising teacher-preparation programs, and developing the kinds of material that would contribute to reaching the goal of economic understanding for all high school graduates.

4. A fourth area of research should be concerned with economics as a body of knowledge. It has certain minimums of fact, analysis, and theory that permit it to be labeled as a discipline. But since economic education is the focus of concern, there must be a mixture of the requirements of the discipline with other educational objectives. The purposes of economic education may vary, and the knowledge necessarily varies with the purpose. Different groups may need different emphases. Does one really know whether the recommendations of the Task Force reach the objective it set for itself?

The entire question of values in education is an important one. Since economics is a behavioral science, the relation of values to the study of economics should be further investigated. Behavioral changes and attitudes may or may not be part of economic education, but, if so, is this the objective of this body of knowledge? Furthermore, with the need for a citizen's understanding of the behavioral sciences, the relation of economics to the other social sciences must be examined.[14,15] Much more needs to be done in examining the relation of economics to social and educational philosophy.[16] Any authoritative decision on whether economics can best be

[14] Hagen, *On The Theory of Social Change, op. cit.*

[15] Donald P. Ray, *Trends in Social Science* (New York: The Philosophical Library, 1961).

[16] Meno Lovenstein, *Economics and The Educational Administrator* (Columbus: College of Education, The Ohio State University, 1958).

learned as a separate discipline or integrated into a variety of courses awaits such evidence.

5. The final area is that of evaluation. A good example can be found in the monograph *Testing Economic Knowledge and Attitudes.*[17] Test construction and test results are examined through a laboratory situation. Admittedly primitive, the study still points the way for the intensive research required. With the proper standardized instruments, special groups can be established for testing many hypotheses. Relationships and comparisons within a school and among schools can be studied. Students can be followed into their later academic careers and their precollegiate work evaluated in terms of later achievement. But evaluative instruments are needed. Is there an adequate explanation of economic understanding? Can comprehension be measured? How can the actions of students be related to their economic understanding? Is there a way to determine economic attitudes? And can relationships be established between all of the above? These are the fruitful areas of study as Wagner sees them.

Of great significance to teaching in this area is the knowledge, attitudes, and value judgments relating to economics that exists in the community, state, and the nation. The development of the school program will move as rapidly and as objectively as the community permits. Identifiable lack of information or misconceptions have to be known and programs developed to overcome these. Ways need to be found to get the support of the community but an inventory of community knowledge will be required first.

The research needed at the collegiate level is perhaps of equal importance. Economic education has not been distinguished from economics. The very questions raised throughout this chapter are equally pertinent to the college level. The question of whether collegiate teaching is as effective as secondary school teaching needs to be determined even for the "scientists" who are the practitioners.

The content in the introductory economics courses, the materials used, the effectiveness of a variety of teaching methods, the correlation between the examinations given and the course objectives, the retention of subject matter, the ability to apply analysis to issues,

---

[17] *Testing Economic Knowledge and Attitudes,* Studies in Economic Education, No. 3. (Iowa City: Bureau of Business and Economic Research, College of Commerce, State University of Iowa, 1955).

the place of values, the attitudes of students and professors, and the grade placement of introductory courses are areas of research needed at the collegiate level.

One of the most significant examinations of needed research in the social sciences was made at a conference at Syracuse University in October, 1963. Discussions were held and significant papers were delivered on "Needed Research on Social Attitudes, Beliefs and Values," "Methods of Research in the Social Sciences," "Sensitizing Students to Fields of Public Policy," "Cultural Background, Attitudes, Knowledge, and Training of Social Studies Teachers," "Psychological Factors in Learning Related to the Social Studies," and "Selection and Organizing of Content for Teaching Purposes."

This conference, held with the support of the U.S. Office of Education, may lead the way toward an investment in research in the social science education programs. Certainly economic education can only benefit by what is done. Abundant suggestions are offered to those who may be searching for the significant areas of study.

The sum of all this is the recognition that much needs to be done to enable those determining the structure and content of the curriculum to move with assurance in developing school programs adjusted to the demands of today's world. A significant program was inaugurated by the Joint Council on Economic Education and its affiliated councils in the fall of 1964.[18] Intensive programs of a three-year duration will be carried on with 30 school systems to develop patterns of curriculum design and to seek a good deal of basic data needed to answer a number of the questions raised in this chapter.

[18] Joint Council on Economic Education Program 1964–1966 (New York: Joint Council on Economic Education, 1964).

Bibliography

Annotated Bibliography of Materials in Economic Education. New York: Joint Council on Economic Education, 1962.

Bond, Floyd A., "Economics, Economists and Educators," *Iowa Business Digest* (March, 1957).

Calderwood, James, *Economic Themes in United States History*. Riverside, Calif.: Office of Riverside County, Superintendent of Schools, 1962.

Chalmers, John and Laurence E. Leamer, "A Philosophy of Economic Education," *The Atlanta Economic Review*, Vol. IX, No. 6 (June, 1959).

Dodd, Harvey J., *et al.*, *Toward Better Economic Education*, Monograph 104. Cincinnati, Ohio: South-Western Publishing Co., November, 1961.

Economics Library Selections, Series 1963–64: New Books in Economics. Pittsburgh: University of Pittsburgh. (Quarterly).

Fersh, George L., "Economic Education," *Education Leadership* (May, 1961).

————, "The JCEE's Decade in Economic Education," *School and Society* (June 30, 1959).

Frankel, M. L., *Changing Emphasis in Social Studies Affecting Curriculum Change* (An address presented at the Annual Meeting of the Minnesota Association for Curriculum Development). New York: Joint Council on Economic Education, November, 1962.

————, "Economic Education For A Free Society," *Iowa Business Digest* (May, 1964).

————, "How Can the Public Schools Do a Better Job of Educating Youth for Economic Literacy?", *Education For World Leadership*, 1960.

————, "Whose Economics Should Be Taught in The High School?" (An Address presented at the Annual Meeting of the American Association of School Administrators, February, 1964). New York: Joint Council on Economic Education, 1964.

Free and Inexpensive Materials For Teaching Family Finance. New York: National Committee for Education in Family Finance, (1963).

Gilliam, J. C., "Economic Education: A Challenge to Business Educators," *The Balance Sheet* (December, 1961).

Hodges, Luther H., "Are We Flunking Economics?," *Vital Speeches* (February 15, 1963).

————, "We're Flunking Our Economic ABC's," *Saturday Evening Post* (March 10, 1962).

Jones, Evelyn, "Survey of Economics in U.S. School Systems in Cities," *Social Education* (January, 1963).

113

Keezer, D. M., "Importance of Economic Education in the Secondary Schools, *National Association of Secondary Schools Bulletin* (May, 1962).

Lewis, Ben W., *Economic Understanding: Why and What* (An address at the American Economic Association Annual Conference). New York: Joint Council on Economic Education, 1956.

Moore, Bessie Boehm, "Economic Education in the Schools," *Delta Kappa Bulletin* (Spring, 1962).

Olson, Milton and Eugene L. Swearingen, "Business and Economic Education for the Academically Talented Students," *NEA Journal* (April, 1962).

Olson, Paul, "The Professional Economist and Economic Education," *Iowa Business Digest* (March, 1957).

Ouellette, Vernon A., "Research in Economic Education," *National Business Education Quarterly* (March, 1960).

Reese, Jim, "The Treatment of Economics in High School American History Texts," *Iowa Business Digest* (March, 1957).

Seagov, Max and Shirley Engle, "Principles of Learning and Teaching Applied to Economics," American Business Education Association (NEA), *American Business Education Yearbook,* Washington, D.C., 1959.

Senesh, Lawrence, "Emerging Patterns of Economic Education in Public Schools," *Iowa Business Digest* (March, 1957).

Suggestions For A Basic Economics Library. New York: Joint Council on Economic Education, 1965.

Teacher's Guide to Economics in the United States, History Course. New York: Joint Council on Economic Education (In preparation).

Teacher's Guide to Economics in World History. New York: Joint Council on Economic Education (In preparation).

Wagner, Lewis E., "Progress in Closing the Materials Gap in Economic Education," *The Bulletin* (March, 1962).

————, "Toward Better Economic Understanding," *Iowa Business Digest* (March, 1957).

Wass, Philmore, "Economic Understanding: An Essential For Teachers," *Teacher Education Quarterly* (Winter, 1957).

Index

Accounting, 86 (*see also* Gross National Product)

American Economic Association, 10 44, 45, 104

American economy (*see* United States)

Banks and banking:
  college courses in money, 98
  credit functions, 7

Behavioral science, 14, 55, 103 (*see also* Economics)

Brookings Institution, report of, on economic education, 108

Business:
  courses, 85, 86, 107
  law, 86
  management, 17,
  organization, 17, 90
  (*see also* History, American; Education, business; Education, economic)

California:
  Contra Costa, 109
  Los Angeles, eleventh-grade unit, 28, 30
  Pomona College, 97, 99
  San Francisco:
    State College, 97
    syllabus for course, 100
  Temple City, 99
  economics program in, 23

Capital, 17, 19, 28
  formation, 81, 82 (*see also* Invesment, capital)

Capitalism:
  government, 19
  private, 19 (*see also* Economic systems)

Cattle industry:
  South and, 77
  study unit on, 39

Centers for Economic Education, 97, 98, 100, 101, 102

Certification (*see* Economics, requirements for certification; Kentucky)

Civics, in ninth-grade, 5, 80 (*see also* Community; civics)

Committee For Economic Development, 104

Communications:
  kinescopes, 94
  media in economics, 16, 45, 57
  radio programs, 5
  TV, films and filmstrips, 94, 105

Community, the:
  civics, 80

contributors to, 2, 38, 40, 76
councils on economic education, 10
and economic activity, 6, 77
eleventh-grade unit, 28
growth, 28
as a laboratory, 6, 16, 41
mathematics, 87
ninth-grade unit, 5, 80
population growth, 2, 30
relationships, 1, 3, 5, 6, 10, 16, 41, 43, 49, 76, 89
resources, 52
role in economic education, 43, 51, 52
role of individual in, 2, 75
school cooperation, 51
second-grade unit, 38

Comparative advantage, 30, 38
  as a concept, 28
  as a theory, 78

Connecticut:
  southern Connecticut, 91, 97
  West Hartford:
    economic growth in, 2, 3
    a sixth-grade study, 2

Councils on Economic Education:
  community, 9, 10
  regional, 9, 10, 31, 43
  State, 10, 43
  (*see also* Joint Council on Economic Education)

Curriculum, 35, 46, 47, 49-54, 56, 74, 75, 87, 88, 92, 98, 100, 101, 104, 110

Democracy, 46, 50, 62, 68
  education and, 60
  problems of (course), 41, 50, 84, 107
  society and, 47

Distribution of income:
  as an historical development, 8
  in United States, 13, 57
  in Western Europe, 25

Economics:
  aggregate, 85
  analysis, 16, 19, 24, 37, 40, 57, 60, 61, 62, 84
  approach to, 49, 51
  as a behaviorial science, 14, 110
  and choice-making, 4, 17
  for citizenship, 56, 105
  in the classroom, 59, 89, 90
  and the community, 76, 110
  competence in, 39, 84
  as a concept, 79, 80, 83, 109
  and the consumer, 84

Geography:
  and economics, 78, 98
  ninth-grade course, 25
  semester requirements, 93
  world, 77
Government, 17, 75, 79, 82, 83, 86
Gross National Product, 9, 22, 30
Growth, economic:
  communist, 78
  conditions, favorable to, 4, 22
  in Connecticut (*see* Connecticut)
  factors of, 3, 9, 28, 81-82
  in New England (*see* Connecticut,
      West Hartford)
  in Paterson, New Jersey, 4
  policy statement on, 8
  social goals and, 82
  and stability, 57, 59, 71, 72, 83, 86,
      91, 106
  as subject of study, 79, 84, 98
  technology and, 83
High school, 38, 39, 48, 54, 87, 108
  Grades 9-12, 99
  students, 45
  teachers, 98
  (*see also* Schools; specific grades)
History:
  analytical approach, 82
  and economics, 79, 84, 98
  and economic understanding, 82, 84,
      107
  in eighth grade, 79
  in eleventh grade, 82
  in fifth grade, 28
  and geography, 79
  requirements for social studies
      teachers, 93
  series of pamphlets, 84
  study of individuals, 79
  study of industrial development, 28
  study of problems, 39, 40
  world, 81
Home economics, 39, 87, 107
Idea relationship, 26, 27, 28, 29
Illinois:
  Center for Economic Education, 101,
      102
  laboratory high school, 85, 100, 101
  University of, 91, 95, 97, 99, 100
  Urbana, 8
  Winnetka, eleventh-grade economic
      unit in, 22
Indiana:
  Purdue University, 95, 97, 100
  Vincennes, tenth-grade study unit,
      21
Individual, 106
  as a citizen, 80
  as a consumer, 80
  relationship to earth, 80
  relationship to life and culture, 80

relationship to world trade, 81
  as a worker, 80
In-service programs, 34, 94, 99, 108
  for teachers, 11, 38, 101
Investment, capital:
  areas needing, 9
  education as an, 34
  profit relationship, 76
  sources of, 8
Iowa:
  comparison with South, 28
  Fort Dodge, 27, 28
  Indianola, 7
Joint Council on Economic Education,
      10, 11, 12, 31, 35, 36, 38, 43,
      44, 84, 98, 100, 101, 109, 112
Junior high school, 39
  (*see also* specific grades)
Labor, 17, 90
Labor economics, 98
Law of diminishing returns, taught in
      second grade, 21
Law of opportunity cost, taught in
      second grade, 21
Massachusetts:
  Boston University, 97
  Newton:
      case study approach, 48
  Wellesley college, 91
Materials, 32, 41, 44, 45, 47, 48, 89,
      94, 99, 100, 101, 103, 104, 110,
      111
  Centers, 100, 101
  Eastern Michigan University, 95
  economic education libraries, 95
  evaluation of, 94, 104, 105, 106
  San Diego, California, library, 95
  supplementary, 108
  for teachers and schools, 35, 43
  use of various kinds of, 42, 48, 49,
      89, 107
Materials Evaluation Committees, 32
Michigan:
  Detroit, 48
  Eastern Michigan University, 95
  economic education in, 1, 41
  Kalamazoo, 1
Minnesota, 98
  "Economics in the News" (radio pro-
      gram), 4
  Minneapolis, 4
  University of, 95, 97
Money, 5
  and banking, 98
  role in the economy, 6, 59, 76
  as a scarce resource, 21
  unit on, in New Haven, 21
Multilateral world trade, 47
National Task Force on Economic
      Education, 32, 33, 37, 38, 44,
      56, 57, 86, 103, 105, 110

New Jersey:
  East Orange, 48
  Montclair State College, 97
    in-service program, 99
  Passaic Valley, and international
    trade, 4
  Paterson, eighth-grade study, 3, 4
  Woodrow Wilson Junior High School,
    Passaic Valley, 4
New York, 24, 28
  program for less-able students, 48
  State Department of Education, 85
  Syracuse University, 90
    research in social sciences, 112
    United States Office of Education
      Project, 112
Ninth-grade, 5, 23, 25, 48, 80, 85
Ohio:
  Akron:
    problems of democracy course, 50
    program for less-able students, 48
  university, 97
Oklahoma:
  State University, 91, 97, 99
  Tulsa:
    Cattle industry study unit, 39
    program for less-able students, 48
Political science, semester-hour re-
    quirements, 93
Problems:
  analytical economic, 19, 22, 24, 25,
    26, 29, 50, 84
  approach in economics, 61, 62, 92
  approach in education, 60, 62
  clusters of, 19
  economic, 57, 59, 62, 65, 78, 80, 82,
    98
  in economic education, 31, 32, 33,
    36
  examples of, 18
  kinds of, 49, 65, 80, 91
  persistent, 17, 18, 19, 20, 106
  socioeconomic, 19, 37
  symptoms of, 19
  in economic education, 15, 61, 90,
    92, 93
Research:
  Bureau of Business, 94
  at the college level, 111, 112
  economic and science, 60, 62
  economic attitudes, 111
  in economic education, 99, 100, 103,
    107, 109, 110, 111, 112, 113
  economic understanding, 111
  and evaluation, 104, 105, 106, 111
  in schools, 35, 54, 88, 92, 96, 111
  in social sciences, 112
Resources:
  allocation of, 13, 54, 56, 57, 69, 76,
    81, 106
  capital, 17, 19, 28, 82

community, 1, 6, 8
conservation of, 40
development of, 6, 30
energy, 47
entrepreneurial, 82
grazing, 18
human, 2, 9, 15, 76, 82
natural, 2, 9, 16, 17, 18, 28, 76, 79,
  82
scarcity of, 5, 14, 21, 22, 27, 39, 64,
  74, 75, 79, 80
South, in the, 28
utilization of, 59, 78
Resources for the Future, Inc., 28
Science, 87
  (see also Social sciences)
Second grade, 1, 21, 38, 54, 75, 76
Seventh grade, 77
Sixth grade, 4, 38, 76
  and Minneapolis unit, 4
  and West Hartford unit, 2
Social studies (or sciences), 55, 103,
  104
  and the curriculum, 40
  at the high school level, 39
  requirements in, 32, 92, 93
  research in, 112
  second grade, 1
  teachers of, 32, 33, 42, 92, 94, 96,
    99
Society:
  decision-making in, 60, 74
  democratic, 47
  freedom in, 17
Sociology, 93
Task Force (see National Task Force
    on Economic Education)
Television courses, 45, 48, 57, 105
Tenth grade, 21, 23, 81, 85
Textbooks:
  economic, 57, 108
  social studies, 105
  use of, 11, 35, 42, 48
Theory, 64, 65, 66, 67
  in economics, 66, 67, 73, 98, 99
Third grade, 76
Trade, international, 109
  in business courses, 86
  European Common Market, 4
Trade, world, 81, 82
  (see also Multilateral world trade)
Twelfth grade, 12, 24, 40, 84, 105, 109
UNESCO, 77
United Nations, 77, 78
United States:
  economy of, 13, 14, 15, 63, 85
  functions of, 22
  problems of 17, 26, 37
Utah:
  Brigham Young University, 97, **100**
  State University, 98

118